MORE THAN

50 WAYS TO BUILD

TEAM CONSENSUS

By

R. Bruce Williams

IRI/Skylight Publishing, Inc.
Palatine, IL

More Than 50 Ways to Build Team Consensus
Second Printing

Published by IRI/Skylight Publishing, Inc.
200 East Wood Street, Suite 274
Palatine, IL 60067
800-348-4474
FAX 708-991-6420

Creative Director: Robin Fogarty
Editors: Julia E. Noblitt, Erica Pochis
Book Designer: Bruce Leckie
Graphic Designer: David Stockman
Type Composers: Donna Ramirez, Liesl Stiegman
Production Coordinator: Amy Behrens

Library of Congress Catalog Card Number 93-078420

Printed in the United States of America.
ISBN 0-932935-48-6

0444B-5-94

CONTENTS

FOREWORD

A fter a lifetime of experience participating on teams as a team
member, team leader, and team builder practitioner, I can safely say
that no leadership area is more prized and valued, more celebrated as an
important key to organizational success, than *teamwork*. Yet, strangely,
no leadership area, in both public and private institutions, is more
misunderstood or more neglected.

In recent years, the drive to improve organizational performance has
been heightened by a number of factors: fierce competition, limited
resources, increased demands for quality, shareholder insistence on better
bottom-line performance, public dissatisfaction with the performance of
their institutions (both public and private), and economic uncertainty.
These are just a few. And, as the pressures for improved performance
have mounted, so too has the focus increased on the importance of
teamwork.

Much is written about teamwork in sports. Much has also been
written about the power of a shared vision to unite people in purposeful
action taking, the value of building consensus, and the commitment
found in collaboration, participation, and interdependence. Yet little has
been written from the point of view of the team coach or practitioner to
help teams build purposeful visions, gain consensus, and achieve the
high-level collaboration and participation required to build true and
meaningful interdependence and commitment.

In *More Than 50 Ways to Build Team Consensus*, R. Bruce Williams
has given us a rich opportunity to achieve these team breakthroughs that
can lead to high-level team performance. I highly recommend this book
to anyone who is a team leader, team coach, or team building practitioner, and even to those team members who wish to learn how to improve
their own team's performance.

X. Daniel Kafcas
President
XDK Associates, Inc.
August 1993

ACKNOWLEDGMENTS

For twenty years, my skills in group facilitation were honed by colleague staff members of the Institute of Cultural Affairs (ICA). Our daily use of participatory, consensus-building methods both internally and externally helped each of us to deepen our attentiveness to the skills and styles which foster group connections. Some of ICA's wisdom in facilitation processes is held in the book *Winning Through Participation* by Laura Spencer which is quoted numerous times in this book. Some of the activities documented in this book came directly from my experiences with ICA. Others, though not coming directly from my experience with ICA, were certainly inspired by my work and training with ICA.

My colleagues at IRI/Skylight have faithfully encouraged the writing of this book. Jim Bellanca is always finding new places and new groups for me to use and model these activities. Within thirty seconds after meeting Robin Fogarty for the first time, she asked me when I would write my book. Kay Burke shows unbridled enthusiasm at each activity I share with her. Beth Swartz takes time and effort to get trained in many of these activities and thereby becomes a witness to their effectiveness from firsthand experience. Beth Forbes and Vicki Sullivan, in their willingness to take on any task, have been critical components of my support. Finally, the staff of Skylight Publishing, at every point, evidence competence and sensitivity in guiding a writer and in transforming the material to make it practical and usable for the reader.

Family and countless friends have patiently followed and enabled the evolution of this book. Jack, Richard, and Jim have surrounded me with support and care that never stops. And I thank my daughter Liz and son Daniel for being there.

INTRODUCTION

S uddenly, a change has occurred in today's workplace. Many people are being called on to manage through teams. With the advent of the necessity to work through teams, tools and strategies to facilitate consensus are called for as never before. There are no easy, clear-cut models to move an organization from top-down, hierarchical decision making to team decisions based on consensus. Consensus tools are needed so that each organization can move ahead into this uncharted future to discern how it will operate.

When tools and strategies are utilized to create a purposeful vision, encourage participative processes, enhance individual commitment, and build a collaborative team, only then can consensus begin to grow. Shortchange any one of these and the consensus is lopsided or incomplete. Without a vision, there is no focus to a consensus and no reason for one. Without participative processes, there is no group road map to work through the intricacies of building consensus meeting after meeting. There is no drive or energy to carry consensus through to completion without individual commitment. Finally, without a unified team, the task of consensus is overwhelming and burdensome. People burn out before consensus is reached.

Building consensus is not an overnight task. It is a process that takes years and can be refined year after year. Nevertheless, you can begin today with your team to set the stage for consensus to grow and to establish an environment that fosters consensus. As you mix tools and strategies from each section of this book, you will create a unique blend of approaches that will move your group toward trust and deep consensus.

ABOUT CONSENSUS

In former eras, one person made a decision and passed it down the chain of command, confident that the decision would be implemented in all the correct places. Today, people are reluctant to carry out a decision in which they have had no voice whatsoever. Furthermore, with increased confidence in their own abilities, people believe they have as much wisdom and as valid a perspective as the person named at the top. Needless to say, this creates an obvious clash between leadership schooled in making top-down decisions and employees who believe their "front-line" wisdom is being ignored. The path out of this perplexity is teamwork with consensus at its heart.

So, what is consensus? Richard Wynn (1984) takes us directly to the dictionary to define the word consensus. He reminds us that the word "consensus" comes from the Latin word "consentire" which means to think together. Wynn goes on to say that the *American College Dictionary* defines *consent* as "general agreement." Based on Wynn's definition, we might say that consensus has something to do with talking and thinking together followed by some form of agreement.

Consensus is both the process people go through to arrive at a mutually agreed-upon decision as well as the product of such a process. People who participate in genuine dialogue over an issue, in the midst of real sharing of a variety of perspectives, are often willing to bend their own private opinions and desires in order to arrive at an effective group decision. That final product is a consensus. The process of thinking together, assuring everyone that each perspective is heard, and moving toward a decision is also a consensus.

When we believe that human beings are motivated solely by pure self-interest, then it is difficult to imagine that consensus can occur. Consensus rests on the assumption that people can voluntarily back off from the aspects of a particular position in order that some aspects of their position can be satisfied in a group agreement. Frank, in Mansbridge's book (1990), suggests that people can care about more than just their own self-interest. Indeed, it is selling human beings short to say that people are motivated only by self-interest.

In addition to whatever drive to self-interest we humans possess, there is also a drive to connect with other human beings. It is this very potential in a human being that is the foundation of the belief in the possibility of consensus. Consensus cannot occur were human beings not able to think and act beyond self-interest alone. The desire to connect is strong. It is the experience of feeling connected that positively motivates even those who are cynical and bitter to try one more time to work with a group of people who are serious about the same issues and concerns.

ABOUT THE SETTING AND LOGISTICS FOR TEAM CONSENSUS
When I am asked to work with a group, several questions come to mind that may also assist you. Does the room have tables and chairs and not just a theater-style arrangement? Does the room have a working wall? Is the group number between ten and fifty? (More than fifty becomes

unwieldy in terms of generating real consensus.) There are other details you will observe as this book unfolds, but these few words may help spur your thinking on some of the basics about setting and logistics.

ABOUT THIS BOOK

Anyone interested in consensus may take this book and read it from cover to cover to gain a full grasp of the consensus process and a multitude of ways to generate consensus in a team. It is also possible to just thumb through to an activity whose title interests the reader and just jump in and use it. The reader may choose to concentrate on only one level, such as the simple or the more difficult strategies.

If your group has just come together for the first time or if your team is a newly constituted team, it might be helpful to delve into the beginning or simpler strategies called Simple Things to Do. If your team has already worked together for several months and performs well with just a few snags, see if some of the medium-level strategies fit your situation (Things That Take Effort). However, for those teams that have been functioning well for quite a while, some of the more advanced strategies may help them to build on their strengths (For the Committed).

This book is also organized into four components of full consensus: Purposeful Vision, Participative Processes, Individual Commitment, and Collaborative Teams. Perhaps your team is manifesting signs that it needs some of the strategies associated with only one of the four major components of this book. If your team is mired in the day-to-day, ongoing, plodding tasks of implementation, some of the strategies of *Purposeful Vision* may help to reinstate the team's awareness of the big picture and revive some of the earlier energy manifested just after the team was constituted.

If your team is argumentative and full of hassling, some of the strategies in *Participative Processes* may help to channel and focus some of your team's energies. Furthermore, if one or two people are dominating your meetings, this section might be particularly useful.

When you find signs that your team or many individuals on your team are refusing responsibility or are allowing only one or two people to do all the work, then your team might be assisted greatly by some of the strategies reviewed in *Individual Commitment*.

Lastly, if your team has strong-willed, competent individuals all pouring much energy into the task but rarely working together, explore the strategies reviewed in *Collaborative Teams*. Our culture has long encouraged strong individual action often to the neglect of helping people operate as a team.

For a review of the theory and the research-base behind some of the concepts used, please read one or more of the sectional introductions. These introductions give the reader some clues about what other experts and practitioners are saying about consensus. The quotes at the beginning of each activity reinforce themes from the whole section.

Needless to say, if an activity does not make any sense for your team at this time, go on to the next one until you find one that clicks with you and your team. Or, if a strategy makes great sense to you but does not go over with the team, go on to another until you find one that works for all of you. Some of the activities are ones you do directly with your group. Others are to help you both before and after your meetings.

You might find it helpful to spend time after you try something to think about what went well, exactly how people felt about what you did, why you think it went well, and how you might improve it the next time you use it. This kind of review and debriefing of yourself can strengthen your capacity and confidence as a facilitator.

Lastly, after you try something, I would be delighted to hear how things are working for you. As you utilize these strategies, you are building teams in places where very few teams have operated before. You are laying tracks for a whole new way of working. Let me know if it worked, how well it worked, if it flopped, and how you have improved on activities.

PURPOSEFUL VISION

"The evidence is growing that certain qualities and norms within work environments promote burnout or inspired performance." (Adams, 1986, p. 96)

People want their actions and efforts to make a difference. The possibility that one's own efforts could really transform something is deeply powerful. On the other hand, cynicism and bitterness result when people sense that anything they do or think has absolutely no effect.

When we talk about consensus, we talk about reviving the hope that actions can result in something positive and affect some genuine change. The despair of our age comes from men and women who have individually been trying to make a difference for years. The issues and problems have grown so large that no one person can make much of a difference anymore. As Peters suggests, "In a time of turbulence and uncertainty, one must be able to take instant action on the front line. But to support such action- taking at the front, everyone must have a clear understanding about what the organization is trying to achieve" (Peters, 1987, p. 398). In other words, unclarity on the vision hampers and stifles action.

Conversely, as Laura Spencer notes, a clear and concrete vision can stimulate and focus concerted action: The Practical Vision "provides the direction toward which an organization can move and align itself. The clearer the vision, the more focused the strategy" (Spencer, 1989, p. 99).

Action that is focused and based on consensus, however, can change many of our deep-seated issues and contradictions. People are beginning to believe that perhaps there is hope in the concerted action of a team. Clearly stating a vision and working collaboratively can create a new setting for profound consensus.

There are environments that promote vision and those that promote burnout. John D. Adams talks about environments that promote inspired performance and vision. Environments that tap into people's hopes and dreams set the stage for powerful consensus. An environment that values individuals allows for creativity, innovation, risk taking, and honest mistakes. In such an environment, inspired minds are valued as much as productive hands.

Environments that promote vision web human beings together in teams so that human minds can be in dialogue with other human minds. One person's visions of possibility are linked with other people's visions of possibility.

An environment of vision places value on human beings and their potential for learning and creativity. Environments that are closed communicate that the answers are already known, eliminate the possibility of human innovation and creativity, and discourage any effort at authentic teamwork. The only thing that is desired in a closed environment is individual obedience and loyalty to the already-decided direction and approaches.

A well-thought-out vision invites action that can only happen with consensus. If a vision is any good, it paves the way for action. The road to action from vision passes through consensus. In other words, action cannot happen without agreement on what to do. If the process just stops with articulating the vision, people soon get the idea that nothing is going to happen. On the other hand, if you create the vision and then dictate exactly how everyone is going to do his or her part, the power of that vision is soon strangled.

The process of creating a purposeful vision together often reveals the hopes and yearnings of all the teammates. People with very different perspectives and job roles suddenly begin to sense their surprising unity with others on the team. Connections are made which heretofore seemed impossible, and the foundation for the process of consensus begins to grow.

If no time is spent on this step of building connections among people, it is unrealistic to expect serious consensus. This is why in today's milieu of instant this and immediate that, it is difficult to convey that the process of consensus does not happen overnight.

People need time to move from an environment of fierce competition to one of connection, cooperation, and consensus.

Once the leaders of an organization have fostered authentic consensus on both the vision as well as the action toward that vision, they can trust that the vision is now shared by all. Following this, if strategies and actions have been genuinely created by everyone out of that vision, then the leaders can trust more and more in the day-to-day implementation of the vision. In this way, authentic consensus permits rapid action and immediate responses.

The process of experiencing consensus is deeply energizing. If you add to this the actual accomplishment of a project, the desire to work and create more successes grows. The potential for deeper and deeper consensus builds as people experience the energizing impact of their work together.

PURPOSEFUL VISION

VISUALIZING THE COMMON DIRECTION

INTRODUCTION TO COMMON DIRECTION

Direction is the end focus, the common picture of where people want to be. People expend energies toward this end product. A common direction funnels people's attention and their endeavors.

Agreement on the focus or direction is critical in setting the stage for consensus. How can there be agreement on the particular steps leading somewhere, if there is no agreement on where you are going? Furthermore, the clearer the picture of the direction, the more potential there is for consensus and the more motivation there is to reach it. Fuzzy pictures of direction only cloud the potential for consensus along the way. Once the common direction has been clearly stated and agreed upon, keeping it visually before people continuously reminds them of the original agreement and thereby increases the trust level among the group.

Simple
Things
To
Do

**PURPOSEFUL
VISION**

*"When you begin with the end
in mind, you gain a different
perspective."*—Covey

Hopes and Desires
Conversation

DESCRIPTION/BACKGROUND

This is a guided conversation during which the participants state in
an informal way what they hope and want for the future of their
organization. If the group is small enough, everyone has a chance to
say something specific about what he or she hopes for. At the
conclusion, the group can name some of the common themes heard
throughout.

Beneath the surface of the day-to-day grind, the nitty-gritty
struggles, as well as the overwhelming issues, lies unarticulated
hopes for the future. These are crowded out so easily by the constant
demands of urgent crises. When hopes and desires finally have a
chance to be articulated, it is extremely easy to identify with them.
Some of them are even deeply spirit-filled and insightful. They raise
the level of the group's thinking and feeling. A short ten-minute
conversation often enables connections among the participants and
adds to the foundation for consensus.

DID YOU KNOW?

- Everyone hopes for something.
- Starting with hopes and desires creates energy; starting with problems and
  complaints saps energy.
- It is easy to forget our deep hopes when the going is rough.

ACTIVITY

#1   *Hopes and Desires Conversation*

You need at least ten or fifteen minutes to do this conversation well. After everyone is seated, suggest to the whole group that you would like to take a few moments to look at the past and the future. Ask the whole group these questions. Try to get four or five responses to each question.

1. What are some of the hallmarks of this past year, or decade for our organization?

2. What are some of your own accomplishments?

3. What are some of your hopes and desires for this organization five years down the road? What do you want to see us become? What do you hope we can accomplish in five years?

4. What have you heard in these responses? What is it we all say we are hoping for?

5. For these desires to be realized, what are some of the concrete implications for us? How we think? How we operate? How we work? How we deal with the community?

Hints ...

✓ Start with questions that focus first on the past. It has been said that people can look ahead only as far as they can look back. As you hear the answers, help the group to make them as specific as possible. There is a large difference between an answer such as "hard economic times" and "the closing of the automobile plant in our town."

✓ Question #4 is crucial. You are helping the group see some of the commonalities in the responses. You are asking the group to connect several responses with a common theme. People can see not only how their ideas are related but how they themselves are related. You are setting the stage for more concrete connections later on.

✓ Question #5 pushes the group in a very nonthreatening way to reveal some of its ideas about the actual implementation of its hopes and desires. Nothing is written down as you lead this, but it can reveal a lot to the leader who is paying attention. Comments here may help you decide what kind of contexts to lay in future meetings. How committed people are and how the group is willing to proceed may also be revealed.

EXAMPLE

When I worked with retail managers from a large department store on creating ways to improve customer satisfaction, some of the responses to the question of what they hoped and desired were:

- Better phone etiquette
- Department product knowledge
- More descriptive signs
- Visible aisle directions
- Weekly employee/employer meetings
- Advertised merchandise always available

After I received fifteen or twenty responses to this question, I asked, "What are some of the common themes you heard running through these responses?" These were some of the common themes they heard:

- On-the-Job Training
- Company Employee Recognition

- Customer Direction Aids
- Improved Service System
- Responsive Sales Force

In just a short time, this group had a sense of its hopes for what it wanted to see happen.

Simple
Things
To
Do

**PURPOSEFUL
VISION**

"Quite simply, the vision must supplant the rule book and policy manual."—Peters

Snapshots

DESCRIPTION/BACKGROUND

When a group has already worked on its vision, instead of having a conversation or a workshop, you can help the members to summarize rapidly what they have done by encouraging small groups of two or three people to draw on chart paper an actual snapshot of some aspect of their vision, hopes, or desires. After the snapshots are collected and shown to the whole group, the group can step back and reflect on the common themes it sees in the pictures and touch base with its vision.

I run into situations where people are sick of doing work on vision. This tells me that while their thinking about their vision is good, it stopped at that point. Because the group did not move beyond the vision, they naturally became disgruntled. A snapshot or picture will seem different from what they have been doing so far.

DID YOU KNOW?

- Kenneth Boulding reminds us that images can be more crucial for change than ideas.
- Pictures can make us think more concretely than words.
- Pictures are the basis of the entire writing system of Chinese characters.

ACTIVITY

#2 *Snapshots*

1. Place some markers, chart paper, and masking tape on each table or with each working team.

2. Have each team create a snapshot or picture on the chart paper that holds and dramatizes some aspect of its vision.

3. Suggest a time limit, such as ten minutes.

4. Have each group choose a reporter.

5. Each team's reporter will present the snapshots to the whole group and put the snapshots on the wall.

6. After all the teams have presented, ask, "What are some of the common themes running through these snapshots?"

7. Have at least ten 5 x 8 cards with borders drawn around them on the wall to record the responses from Question #6, one response per card.

Hints . . .

✓ **Assorted colors of markers for each team increase motivation.**

✓ **Repetitious pictures do not matter, and gaps in the total picture of the snapshots are O.K. You are honoring the dimension of vision here, you are not after comprehensiveness at this point.**

✓ **My experience is that this provides a way for people to talk about their hopes and visions so quickly that their cynicism does not have a chance to show itself.**

✓ **Another advantage to this activity is that it structures in concreteness. If you are drawing a picture you have to have specifics in mind. The very concreteness of the pictures provides points for real agreement and consensus among the participants.**

EXAMPLE

Often I am called on to work with groups who have spent months and months trying to hammer out their vision. The more the months progressed, the more discouraging and frustrating the process felt. By the time I was asked to lead one group, it was almost too late.

After giving a social agency fifteen minutes to come up with pictures, their pictures showed:

- Newer equipment
- Satisfied clients
- Staff working in teams around a table
- A newsletter
- More diverse clients
- Attractive marketing and public relations materials
- Staff getting new training
- Staff working and planning with the board

Out of this abbreviated sampling, perhaps you can see how easy it was to discern common themes such as:

- Effective Public Relations
- Accessible Consumer Services
- Consistent Financial Development
- Multidirectional Communication
- Positive, Proactive Board Development

#3

PURPOSEFUL VISION

"The skill of visioning underlies each of the key elements of creating inspired perfor-mance."—Jaffe, Scott, Orioli, from Adams

Brainstorming Closure

DESCRIPTION/BACKGROUND

As it is helpful during a meeting for participants to see, as well as hear, the deliberations or the brainstorming, many facilitators use chart paper to record ideas brainstormed by the group. Very often, however, people do not know what to do once they have made a brainstormed list. The ideas just stay there and go nowhere.

Brainstorming Closure suggests that once you acquire a brain-stormed list you enable the group to step back and discern the points of agreement appearing through the entire list.

DID YOU KNOW?

- Many facilitators are good at brainstorming—not many are good at knowing what to do with brainstorming.
- Sometimes it is not more data people need but how to organize and deal with the data they already have.
- Thirty pieces of information feel overwhelming to a group—seven or eight major themes seem possible to handle or respond to.

A C T I V I T Y

#3

Brainstorming Closure

1. Ahead of time, prepare the questions for the group to brainstorm, such as:

    a. What are different ways we can market this product?

    b. Where are possible places to cut the budget?

    c. What are steps we can take to improve employee participation and loyalty?

    d. What are some simple ways we can use to increase customer service?

2. After individuals have time to jot down their own responses, have teams of two, three, or four talk through some of their ideas.

3. Then ask, "What are some of the responses your teams talked about?"

4. Record all the ideas mentioned on chart paper, attempting to get a list of fifteen to twenty ideas.

5. Next to the chart paper have eight to ten blank 5 x 8 cards in a vertical column.

6. Read the brainstormed list and ask the group what the major themes or major points of agreement are.

7. Write these points, one per card, on the cards lined up next to the chart paper.

8. Conclude by asking the group a question to help it process this information, such as:

    a. What insights has this data generated for you?

    b. What do you see are our next steps?

    c. What implications come out of this?

Hints . . .

✓ If you directly open the question to the whole group, you are inviting only those quick thinkers or those with axes to grind to begin the discussion.

✓ If people get stuck, read over the answers to generate more responses.

✓ If you have time, a fuller workshop such as that suggested in Cardstorming is better. (See Activity #7.) If all you have is twenty minutes, this is an ideal way to get lots of ideas and bring the ideas into some kind of focus.

✓ Note that the "points of agreement" referred to in question #6 are not individual items chosen from the brainstorm list but represent combinations of items or the item behind several items on the list.

EXAMPLE

At a recent conference, I asked people, "What do you see going on in a school moving toward 'new vision, new action?'" (the theme of the conference). In the brainstormed list, I got such responses as:

> More teams
> People asking questions
> Clear guidelines
> Restructuring teams
> Staff meeting with community
> Student-centered classrooms
> Students working in groups together

When I asked the question of common themes appearing throughout the whole list, the responses often became much more thoughtful:

> Action Groups
> Student-Parent-Community Involvement
> Consensus Decision Making
> Conflict Resolving and Problem Solving
> Empowered People

#4

"The most powerful, driving, unifying visions share several qualities: 1. They are concrete and specific; 2. They are bold, challenging and exciting; 3. They are attainable."—Spencer

TV Personality in Three Years

DESCRIPTION/BACKGROUND

In a guided conversation, participants will be able to clearly imagine or visualize the future. Using a TV news personality and a cameraperson, you can dramatize the kind of concrete imagining you want the participants to do. Possible responses like "people taking more responsibility" are replaced with "weekly team meetings" or "posted team reports."

By asking people to concentrate on what they can actually see several years down the road, you make their ideas more practical and concrete. This activity moves people beyond the intellectual statement of goals to a realistic imagining of what the goal would look like in practice.

DID YOU KNOW?

- When people imagine, they start to tap into additional parts of the brain than when they are just doing linear thinking (logical, step-by-step thinking).
- Seeing is believing.
- Taking people out of the present moment and down the road three years unclutters their imaginations from the day-to-day problems and concerns.

ACTIVITY

#4   *TV Personality in Three Years*

1. Have the group choose a national or local TV news personality who will do a special report three years from now on your organization highlighting some successful resolutions to the concerns discussed in this meeting.

2. Be sure to include the cameraperson to remind people of the necessity of the visual.

3. Suggest people put down their pens and pencils. To encourage imagining, they might look out the window or at the ceiling or even close their eyes. By giving them permission to imagine, you are tapping that dimension of the brain which can release some genuine creativity.

4. Since each person is hosting a news personality and the cameraperson, he or she is choosing what to include on the video presentation.

5. You might guide people through the areas or places the camera might visit: "Take our visitors first to a staff meeting. What will they see going on?" or "As our visitors walk through the offices, what will the camera capture on the walls that indicates something new is going on?"

6. When people have had a few minutes to do this kind of imagining, bring them back to the present, suggesting that they write down the things they have just imagined.

7. After they have had a chance to write, have groups of three or four share their responses for a few minutes.

8. Ask the whole group to mention the things their small groups talked about.

9. Finally, to close, you might ask, "What are some of the common themes running through our responses?"

Hints . . .

✓ I encourage people to close their eyes at the beginning. I even joke that this is the only time during our work together that I will ask people to close their eyes. At the end of this imagining time, I sometimes clap my hands to symbolize that we are returning to the present.

✓ Do not worry if you hear some wild ideas. Remember, your ultimate goal is to discover some of the common areas of thought.

✓ Very often, people are astounded at how similar their envisioning is. You are linking people's minds and hearts together when you provide connections with what they want in the future.

✓ Make this a full workshop by shifting immediately to Cardstorming (Activity #7) or Brainstorming Closure (Activity #3).

EXAMPLE

Whenever I lead the practical vision workshop in a planning session, I include the TV news personality activity as the first step of individual thinking. After this, I have individuals write down the things they saw. This then provides grist for the team's sharing time.

When I did this activity with a group concerned about home health services, they came up with responses like these:

- A vitalized, strategic plan
- Maximized cash flow
- Low employee turnover
- Consistent policies and procedures
- Patient satisfaction
- Community recognition
- Enhanced management skills
- Confident management team
- Kindred spirit "We are one"

When we pulled it all together, these were some of the common overall themes or titles for the clusters of responses:

- Quality Patient Care
- Responsive Planning
- Strong Stable Staff
- Cultivated Growth
- Financial Solvency

Simple
Things
To
Do
PURPOSEFUL
VISION

"Today, in some of our most successful companies, a few visionary leaders ... have discovered a powerful tool for capturing the spirit and energy of their organizations: the vision statement."—Richards, Engel, from Adams

Common Direction Written Summary

DESCRIPTION/BACKGROUND

This writing exercise allows participants to get down in print their own understandings of the common direction. This can happen after a conversation or workshop. Each group of two or three writes its own interpretation of the common direction. Then, upon hearing each team's paragraph, the whole group can build one common statement of the direction.

Once the conversation or workshop has articulated the elements of the common direction, there still needs to be a way to see how all the major elements are tied together or related. A writing exercise such as this helps to perform that function.

This is another opportunity for creativity and genius to show forth. And indeed, when it does show forth, people are deeply appreciative of each other's thinking. When appreciation occurs naturally, such as in an exercise like the written summary, more connections and ties occur that set the stage for deeper consensus as the team continues to work together.

DID YOU KNOW?

- Writing makes your workshop product available to those who were not present.
- Writing often connects the pieces of your vision into one continuous fabric.
- The process of writing helps people make the common directions their own.

ACTIVITY

#5

Common Direction
Written Summary

1. Review with the group the major elements of the common direction as discussed or worked on in a preceding workshop (e.g., "We have said that these six areas are part of our vision").

2. Break up into teams of three or four people.

3. Suggest that each team compose one paragraph to summarize and interrelate all the elements of the common direction. Give them about fifteen minutes. In addition, have them make a pictorial representation of the common direction. While they are working, they must choose a reporter to share their paragraphs and pictures.

4. After each team has completed its paragraph and pictorial representation, have each team present them. Clap or show acknowledgment after each presentation. I suggest that the groups put their work on chart paper so that they can see the work for themselves.

5. Because the paragraphs are up front on chart paper, it will be easy for the group to discern the elements and pieces that state the common direction. You can begin to build a whole-group statement of the common direction in this way.

6. When you are finished, ask how their understanding of the common direction expanded or changed during this activity.

Hints . . .

✓ **Having all the necessary materials present is critical to the success of any activity.**

✓ **To help with the pictorial representation, chart paper and assorted colors of markers will encourage the teams.**

✓ **You might suggest that they use this simple format for their paragraphs: an introduction, a sentence about each element, and a concluding statement.**

EXAMPLE

In one Chicago public school, a team chosen by the local school council asked me to initiate a process to achieve consensus on relieving overcrowding at their school. After the team discerned the major events to the process and put all these steps on a timeline, it decided to articulate what its bottom-line goals were. When they wrote the goals out, they saw that each goal could be stated in one word. So for weeks afterward, they could say just three words (Values, Process, and Facility) and remind themselves of the entire goal statement. In fact, they even took the first letter of each one (V, P, and F) and created a catchy slogan—Very Positive Future.

The following are the three goal sentences this group came up with. Notice that values is in the first goal, process in the second, and finally, facility in the third.

GOALS

I.   To ensure our *values* are held in the solution.

II. To foster the growth of a *process* that involves the diverse community.

III. To develop a plan for optimizing the use of current and potential *facility*:
   A. Systems and organizational change
   B. Reconfiguring and restructuring facility and space
   C. Expand current facility or acquire more space

#6

Simple
Things
To
Do

**PURPOSEFUL
VISION**

"Mythos is the mechanism through which the group comes to experience its past, present and potential."
—Owen

Past, Present, and Future Images

DESCRIPTION/BACKGROUND

This short activity has three parts. First, the group does a whole-team brainstorm on the past, present, and future of the organization or the team itself. After enough ideas have been generated about its past, present, and future, the group divides into three mini-teams to make a pictorial or graphic image of the past, present, or future. Finally, each mini-team presents its product to the whole group. A processing question will help them reflect on what happened during the exercise.

Daily urgent issues and concerns often crowd out the long-range perspective, making it difficult for a group to recall where it has come from and why it is meeting. This short activity will not only tap people's creativity and imaginations, but also remind them of the bigger picture, to give broader meaning to the tasks of the moment.

DID YOU KNOW?

- Setting the moment into the larger historical flow reminds the group that other crisis moments have been survived.
- Seeing the whole picture can put the team into a mental position to see new solutions for current issues.

ACTIVITY

#6

Past, Present, and Future Images

1. Set a context about why it is important for all of us to keep the long-range goals and the big picture in mind.

2. Have three pieces of chart paper taped on the front wall or blackboard labeled: PAST, PRESENT, and FUTURE.

3. Have people do some individual thinking about phrases, ideas, or images to put in any of the three areas. Ask them to jot down ideas or images under each category.

4. After three minutes, list the ideas or images on the chart paper under their appropriate category.

5. When all three pieces of chart paper have been filled, divide the group into three mini-teams. Have each team work on either the past, present, or future.

6. Give each team several minutes to come up with a picture or graphic representation of its assigned time period.

7. When each mini-team is through, have the mini-team share its picture or image with the whole group. Acknowledge or recognize each presentation in some way.

8. Ask one or two processing questions at the end, such as:

   a. "What happened to your mini-team as you worked on this?"

   b. "What insights came to you?"

   c. "What happened to your own thinking as you heard each report?"

Hints . . .

✓ **The mood during this activity can be very upbeat. The steps can go fairly rapidly.**

✓ **This activity could also be the first step to writing a whole story based on the ideas brainstormed under the PAST, PRESENT, and FUTURE. Each team would only need to write a paragraph on its section. Having this read can be a powerful and affirming event.**

EXAMPLE

In working with a division of an airline company, after they had brainstormed ideas and images for their past, present, and future, they decided to actually write a brief story, doing a paragraph on each. This is the written summary of their past, present, and future.

Higher Horizons

Remember when we were kids? And how Mom and Dad protected us? Our business and our company were much like that. The Government protected and made sure we all did the same thing. We were managed in a parent/child style. Everything was thought about and done for us. Each experience was new; exciting for you, as well as the customer. Flying was an event. Each event got bigger and faster…DC4, DC8, 747.

As a child, we lived in a protected neighborhood. As we entered into the '80s and adolescence, we grew in size and became a little smarter. We experimented, we began to leave the neighborhood. Kids came into our neighborhood. Sometimes, we got a bloody nose. But the real challenges were to our intellect. The old values were not so clear-cut. Technology advances were not in the size and speed of aircraft, but on systems that benefited the customer. Earning money became the most important value. Living and everyday decisions became more complex. We found ourselves on the brink of maturity.

Over a period of fifty years, we have had the opportunity to look at a rich childhood and an adolescence that stimulated intellectual growth. Our experience has prepared us for uncertain yet exciting times. We are confident that by leading and involving our people, we will all move to higher horizons.

**PURPOSEFUL
VISION**

CREATING VISIBLE
DOCUMENTATION

INTRODUCTION TO DOCUMENTATION

Documentation makes the results of any team meeting visible. It gets people's good thinking on paper for all to see—both right at the moment in a temporary fashion as well as a more permanent record soon after the meeting has ended. While we tend to forget the details of what went on, we often remember the things we like or the things closest to our own thinking. Documentation reminds us of the whole picture.

It is the clear picture that propels us forward. The clear vision keeps us moving day to day with its often anxiety-producing details. When you have points of consensus around the vision, you can build on those consensus connections as you implement your goals. Returning from time to time to the vision (which you have permanently documented) reminds people not only that there have been many points of consensus already, but that it is possible to reach consensus even during a particularly controversial issue.

24

Things
That
Take
Effort
**PURPOSEFUL
VISION**

*"When any work team or
division sees how their new
project or task matters, they feel
excited to call on more of their
abilities and energy."* —Jaffe,
Scott, Orioli, from Adams

Cardstorming

DESCRIPTION/BACKGROUND

Many people use chart paper on a regular basis to record brainstormed ideas. During the course of any meeting, it is crucial for
participants to see, as well as hear, the content of deliberations or
brainstorming. It is also possible to use cards, particularly when you
are delving into new ideas and want to get a sense of the clusters of
data under consideration.

Most meetings become discussions among the involved or most
involved personalities. Keeping the information before you on cards
enables an authentic dialogue with the data. As with chart paper, it
keeps the focus on the data and not on particular personalities. The
advantage of recording data on 5 x 8 cards is the flexibility you have
in organizing the ideas later to see the connections.

DID YOU KNOW?

- Utilizing both verbal and spatial intelligences (and others) is a major step
  toward becoming more creative.
- Howard Gardner has identified seven major intelligences: verbal/linguistic,
  logical/mathematical, bodily/kinesthetic, musical/rhythmic, visual/spatial,
  interpersonal, and intrapersonal.
- Making people's thinking visible helps the group appreciate its own value.
- The discussions that occur in this activity are critical for discovering a group's
  consensus.

ACTIVITY

#7 *Cardstorming*

1. Ahead of time, prepare the question for the group to brainstorm.

2. Set a short context with the group, indicating why it is particularly relevant to deal with this question at this time.

3. After posing the question, give people time to do their own thinking. That way, both the quick and the careful thinkers have ample time to organize their thoughts.

4. Suggest that teams of two, three, or four (depending on the size of your whole group) talk through some of their ideas. This gives people "air time" in small groups, permitting some early feedback to their ideas and relieving some of the need to use whole-group time to air their ideas.

5. In the small teams, have people write their ideas on the 5 x 8 cards, one idea per card, using just three to four words per card. Suggest a total number of cards needed from each team.

6. Ask each team to pass up one or two cards, e.g., "Pass up your most clear card first." Tape these on the wall at random.

7. To get a sense of the breadth of the group's thinking, ask them to pass up a card that is most different from anything on the wall so far.

8. Ask the group if they see connections among the cards. Cluster only the cards the group suggests are connected.

9. When clusters begin to emerge, ask the group to come up with a temporary title for the cluster. For example, if you have cards that say "meetings more organized," "shorter meetings," and "clearer memos," the group may cluster those and assign the title, "Communication."

10. Label the clusters with a number, letter, or symbol.

11. Call for the remaining cards, suggesting that people write the number, letter, or symbol on the card if it naturally fits a cluster already up front.

12. Cards can be shifted and moved from cluster to cluster as you get greater clarity with more and more cards coming to the front.

13. Once all the cards have been clustered, go back and clarify and polish the title for each cluster.

Hints . . .

✓ Tape loops are helpful ways to attach cards to a wall. To save time, prepare some tape loops in advance.

✓ It is useful to get thirty to forty pieces of information all together.

✓ Be sure to have the team members write in large letters on the cards.

✓ If you immediately open the question to the group, bypassing the small-team step, you are inviting only the quick thinkers or those with axes to grind to begin the discussion.

✓ I keep 3 x 5 Post-it notes handy to jot down the temporary titles for the clusters of cards.

✓ Make sure you ask the group where to put a card. It is tempting to place the cards where you as leader think they should go.

✓ Think ahead of time what you need this information for and prepare one more question to help the group use the information that it has just generated. Asking a question about the implications or the next steps gives people a chance to see the value in their thinking together. For example, "What insights has this data generated for you?" "What are our next steps?" "What are the implications for us or for you?" "Which ideas have most appealed to you?"

EXAMPLE

In my work with a publishing company, we used cardstorming to help them see aspects of their five-year vision. Here are three of their clusters of ideas and images for their future.

Flexible, Responsive Personnel/Work Environment	Multimedia, Multilingual Products	Proactive Marketing and Sales Focus
Larger Staff	Laser Discs	Four-Color Catalog
5 Project Teams	Interactive Video and Audio Training	International Markets
Employee-of-the-Month Award	On-Line Networking	Foreign Rights Legal Department
Employee Input into Goal Setting	Books in Color	Marketing Department
Permanent Wall Dividers	Publish Kid Books	Test Marketing Program

#8

PURPOSEFUL
VISION

"To begin with the end in mind means to start with a clear understanding of your destination. It means to know where you're going so that you better understand where you are now and so that the steps you take are always in the right direction."—Covey

Meeting Products Documentation

DESCRIPTION/BACKGROUND

Each meeting needs to be planned with a specific product in mind. Getting that product down on paper, copied, and distributed before or at the next meeting is a specific way of making the team's thinking visible and declaring to the team that meeting time is valuable because the product is worth documenting and printing.

Making thinking visible is a critical aspect of thinking clearly. One reason group discussion often goes on ad nauseam is that the thinking has not been documented or written down, and people repeat what has already been said. In addition, when you document the meeting products and make them available you are creating a history of the team piece by piece. Such a clear picture of a team's past enables that team to continue to move forward with clarity and focus.

DID YOU KNOW?

- Seeing our work in print makes us feel it is worthwhile.
- Definite meeting products remind us that our time has been well spent.
- Getting our work documented helps counteract our human tendency to forget our accomplishments.

ACTIVITY

#8 *Meeting Products Documentation*

Many of the activities in this book are suggestions for what you might do before or after a meeting. This one suggests things to do both before and after the meeting.

1. Careful thought before each meeting is necessary to determine what the real product will be. If you cannot discern a product, perhaps you need to think through once more what the purpose of the meeting is.

2. If the product is a decision, documenting the critical elements of the discussion, the possible options, or the stated values that went into the decision may be all that is needed.

3. A record of the meeting products is invaluable when it comes time to make periodic reports or if an article is needed on what has been going on.

4. This kind of printed record also can cut down on discussions or dis-agreements about what was decided or how something was decided.

5. Distributing this product to each person present at the meeting affirms the value of each person.

6. After each person has a chance to look at the product from the previous meeting I might ask:

    a. What do you notice now after seeing this in print?

    b. What are some of the messages this product communicates?

    c. What changes would you make to improve this?

Hints . . .

✓ Writing down things that are discussed on chart paper or cards will be helpful when you print the meeting product to hand out at the next meeting.

✓ Having such documentation will help to fill in the person absent and enable fuller participation from that person during the meeting following the absence.

✓ If you have not been able to finish the product in one meeting, I suggest either printing exactly how far you have gotten toward the product or keeping the chart paper used, bringing that half-finished paper back to the next meeting.

✓ If as facilitator you have difficulty leading the meeting and writing things down at the same time, have one of the team members do that job while the meeting is going on. That person can both participate and write things down for everyone to see.

✓ For meetings that last a couple of days, you may want to have someone right there typing things as the meeting progresses. While some might consider that annoying to meeting partici-pants, it adds a fine sense of drama, especially if people sense they are going to get this material—perhaps even before they leave the meeting to return home.

EXAMPLE

For seven months I worked with a team to create a community consensus on an issue facing a school. There was at least one clear product from each of the weekly meetings held. These products were each typed, copied, and distributed at the following meeting. Some of these products included:

- Six-month plan
- Narration or description of the phases of our plan implementation
- List of team members (how we divided the group into sub-teams)
- Brainstorm on elements of an effective team, a team that works
- The meeting flow of a workshop the team was planning
- Values we wanted our task results to hold
- Three broad goals/objectives for the team
- List of solution options
- Three broad solution scenarios

"The sense of personal power, the belief that one can make a differ-ence, is one of the key elements in inspired performance, and in determining personal health."
— Jaffe, Scott, Orioli, from Adams

Artifacts

DESCRIPTION/BACKGROUND

Traditionally, verbal reports are used to give information about how things are going. Another way to give information is to bring con-crete objects that represent some aspect of the things that are going on. Objects associated with projects and accomplishments help make what you are saying very real. If you are leading several teams, you might even suggest that for the next meeting each team bring at least one "artifact" to represent one of its accomplishments. Again, this communicates that when we say "implementation" we mean that real, concrete events with actual results are expected.

Some people do get very clear pictures from words. Some people even get very clear pictures from a page of numbers. Other people need to see and feel concrete objects. Furthermore, it is harder for the cynics among us to deny concrete objects since words and numbers can easily be fabricated or made to exaggerate what really happened. There is an "undeniability" that surrounds concrete artifacts. Artifacts become proof that the vision previously articu-lated has become a reality.

DID YOU KNOW?

• Sometimes we do not "get it" until we see it.
• Concrete products and artifacts help convince even the strongest doubters among us.
• Seeing someone else's use of an idea sparks a creative way we can use the same principle.

ACTIVITY

#9 *Artifacts*

1. If you are meeting with a number of teams, each team can present its artifact with a brief description.

2. Following each presentation, initiate some appropriate recognition, such as applause or a word of appreciation.

3. After all the teams have made a presentation, be sure to ask one or more of these processing questions to the entire group:

   a. Which artifact do you remember?

   b. Which ones did you like particularly?

   c. What is the message communicated through all of these artifacts?

   d. What are some of our learnings in the process of accomplishing all of these?

4. This same flow could occur with just one team present, asking each person to present an artifact from his or her recent work.

Hints . . .

✓ As the leader, encourage the presentations to be brief—one to two minutes. The artifact itself is the message.

✓ If all team members did not bring a concrete object, give them a moment to draw a picture or put something on paper to represent the project or accomplishment they wish to report on.

✓ The processing questions are particularly important for they help people to internalize the fact that things are happening. There is no better way to impact the remaining doubters than with real success.

✓ Some people may have some negative learnings. "I'll never do this in this situation again, but I might do it in that one." "If I do it again, this is how I would modify it to guarantee different results." These are very valuable learnings. They acknowledge that not everything tried works perfectly.

EXAMPLE

When an organization providing home health care decided to meet to plan its second year, I suggested the employees bring some artifacts to the meeting. Posters for their fund-raising benefit, T-shirts with the name of their organization, items from a booth they staffed at a town fair, articles in the paper, tickets to benefit performances, and artwork from clients all started to fill the table. Seeing all those artifacts imbued everyone with such a tremendous sense of success that they jumped into the planning of their second year.

Things
That
Take
Effort

PURPOSEFUL VISION

#10

"People need to feel that what they are doing is meaningful and important and to connect that work with the overall work of the organization, and that what the company does matters to the world in some way."
—Jaffe, Scott, Orioli, from Adams

Report

DESCRIPTION/BACKGROUND

Preparing a report for someone outside the larger group can be very motivating. It pushes the team to clearly articulate what they have been doing to work toward the vision and the goals. This can be an opportunity to pull together several pieces of things that have been going on to create an integrated picture of it all. Very often the team is surprised to discover all that has happened.

Reporting to someone outside can initiate valuable processing and reflection about what has happened so far and what the next steps need to be. It is a way to step out of the day-to-day implementation pressure and take stock of how well things are going and what kind of improvements can be made. This is particularly helpful when the outside person is encouraging, insightful, and knows how to offer meaningful recommendations and reflections which reveal that the report has been studied carefully and is appreciated.

DID YOU KNOW?

- Just knowing you are going to make a report makes you work even harder to make things happen a little better.
- Making a report is one way of standing accountable to your project.
- Preparing a report assures people that their vision is becoming a reality.

#10 *Report*

I have already suggested that getting things written down and documented is one way to keep your team's vision alive and growing. Making a report is a variation on this theme. Presenting a report can be a high-energy event.

1. The key is that everyone on the team gets into the act of preparing the report.

2. A short, team workshop (using Cardstorming in Activity #7) could help pull together the structure of the report.

3. The structure can help determine how to divide the responsibility for pulling the report together.

4. Again, gathering concrete artifacts is critical. Pictures, charts, graphs, comparisons, third-party documentation, articles, etc., all help the person to whom you are reporting get a rapid grasp of what has been accomplished.

5. If possible, use a team member and not the team leader to present the report. This helps to symbolize that the accomplishments belong to the whole team.

Hints . . .

✓ **If your team has done a faithful job of documenting all the products from your meetings, the report pull-together will not be difficult.**

✓ **A simple, one-page report is perfectly acceptable—and may be easier to understand than a complex, twenty-page document.**

EXAMPLE

The time came for a school subcommittee to report to the entire local school council. It would have been possible to just give the council the particular recommendations we had come up with. However, the subcommittee became very involved in making this report. Before I knew it, they had pulled together a history leading up to this issue, some critical factual data, a record of our planning and training processes, all of the data gathered from the various stakeholders during focus group input sessions, as well as the analysis the subcommittee had made leading to our recommendations. The subcommittee compiled an amazingly complete report, far beyond my expectations. The subcommittee then used that report opportunity to get feedback from the council relative to its next steps. The entire twenty-five minutes became an upbeat event rather than a boring report.

11

Things
That
Take
Effort

**PURPOSEFUL
VISION**

*"Effective visions are lived in
details, not broad strokes."*
—Peters

Wall Decor of
Meeting Products

DESCRIPTION/BACKGROUND

The decision-making process is greatly enabled when relevant
meeting products are kept on the wall so that meeting participants
can constantly refer to them. This may be no more than three or
four sheets of chart paper with the relevant discussion points of the
last meeting written on them.

Keeping meeting products on the wall forces the attention of
team members on the issues at hand. It keeps thinking on track as
the group moves toward consensus, and it keeps the actualization of
the vision continuously in view.

It is important to communicate to individuals that their ideas are
important. Team members look on the wall and see that an idea
they mentioned last week is still there. People do not have to keep
proving themselves because their contributions are visible and
continually referred to as meetings progress. When team members
walk into the room and see the products posted on the wall, suddenly the space becomes theirs (even if it is not always theirs).

DID YOU KNOW?

- Being surrounded by the products of hard work can provide the kind of
  energy stained glass windows provide people who enter Gothic cathedrals.
- Posted meeting products remind us that our team is winning.
- Seeing our past meeting products helps us focus on where we are headed in
  the future.

ACTIVITY

#11 *Wall Decor of Meeting Products*

This activity involves your time before and after the meeting, and it concerns your meeting space. With this activity, you are setting the stage for the drama of your meeting.

1. As you think through the flow and the products needed at the next meeting, think back on past discussion material and meeting products to determine which will be the most useful for the next meeting.

2. Arriving a few minutes before the meeting can give you time to put those pieces of paper on the wall before people get there. In doing this, you are claiming that space for your team even if only for the hour you are meeting together.

3. More than likely this space is not only for your team, so it will be necessary to remove everything between meetings.

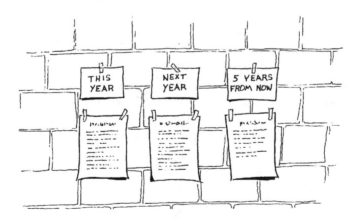

Hints . . .

✓ I suggest that even after you type up a meeting product from a previous meeting, keep that material to post on the wall at the next meeting. Gradually, as material is no longer relevant to current discussions or a future meeting, it can be removed.

✓ You might store meeting products for a while, as you never know whether something will be needed for an unexpected discussion three or four weeks down the road.

✓ Remove the masking tape each time you take the paper down to avoid the tape sticking to several of your sheets and thereby damaging them.

✓ The extra time you spend putting up and taking down these previous meeting products can possibly reduce the time spent explaining something already discussed at length.

EXAMPLE

I met with one group for several months. Unfortunately, we sometimes met in a different space each week. I would get there fifteen minutes ahead of time each week so that I could not only lay out the materials for the current meeting, but also put up the particular previous meeting products which would be useful for that meeting.

I sensed that since there was so much change in the area of our meeting spaces, the consistency of the wall products would be helpful.

As the focus of each meeting shifted, I chose only the previous meeting products which had relevance to the particular focus of that meeting.

"After the vision is written, a visionary must be prepared to spend considerable time, thought, and energy helping to make it happen." —Richards, Engel, from Adams

Article

DESCRIPTION/BACKGROUND

This activity promotes the creation of an article on some aspect of the team's work that will appear in a local publication or the organization's internal publication. Articles like this do not need to be very long; pictures, graphs, or charts can add to the impact.

People who sense that their work is going to be on stage tend to put additional energy and focus into the accomplishment of the task. A lot of us get additional excitement about our work if we know that people outside are going to learn about it. By translating the hard work of a team into an article, you are helping "tell the story." This all adds to sustaining the purposeful vision as it continues to unfold.

DID YOU KNOW?

- Writing an article declares some good news to those around us.
- Sharing our work in an article may help to change someone else's mood for the better.
- Writing an article creates pride in the whole team.

ACTIVITY

#12 *Article*

1. Have the team decide how often an article needs to be in a local or internal publication.

2. Making a brainstormed list of possible articles or what can go into each article can help utilize the whole team's wisdom.

3. If there is a person or two who is gifted in writing and want to send articles to the local publication, encourage this.

4. Otherwise, spreading this assignment around to pairs of people on the team is another way to go.

5. Or, the team may decide to devote a little time before each article is due to create the article as a whole team.

6. Be sure to display the articles and make mention of them.

Hints . . .

✓ Simplicity that leads to regularity is more important than one massive effort that never occurs again.

✓ Deciding on the particular focus of each article as a team each time may make it easier to remember why the whole writing effort is important.

✓ A similar impact on the team can occur if one of the team accomplishments makes it to a news spot on TV. This kind of attention and recognition can go a long way in sustaining the work level and motivation of the team.

EXAMPLE

Seven months after a planning and implementation session that created Partnership Projects to foster business-education partnerships, an article appeared in the local Sunday paper excerpted below:

"School children can count on having a lot more face-to-face contact with business people during the coming year.

Business, industry and labor leaders are taking a personal interest in what is going on in the classroom because they realize they have an important contribution to make toward improving the work force of the future. . . .

Although the focus is in the grade schools at this time, the program will be eventually phased into the secondary schools.

"Business and industry partners are being asked for a different kind of involvement than in the past. . . .

Also, gourmet partnerships have been started. Certain restaurants are hosting, at no charge, lunch for an elementary school principal, student, teacher, parent, and a business person of the school's choice.

The purpose of these luncheons is to establish a dialogue between the schools and business and by the end of the school year every elementary school will have an opportunity to participate. . . ."

This team came up with an ingenious idea, let the whole community know about it, and increased support and commitment for its work.

PURPOSEFUL VISION

ILLUMINATING THE TOTAL FRAMEWORK

INTRODUCTION TO THE FRAMEWORK

People hunger to see the whole picture; they are lost without some sense of the total framework. Too often when we delegate only slices of the whole pie, the old framework falls apart and no longer makes sense. People need to build a new framework that puts the purpose-filled vision in a broader context. Purposeful vision provides the why of daily actions and offers the full story behind that vision. People who are enabled to see the total framework can become more willing participants in the implementation of the vision.

Consensus on the total framework is a foundational step to creating consensus on various action strategies. In fact, consensus on the total framework can release creativity in the mapping of implementation strategies. Illuminating the total framework opens people's consciousness to a new level releasing unexpected energy toward the desired outcomes. In this way, the total framework begins to tap the profound commitment of a group so critical to the group's authentic consensus.

"Effective visions prepare for the future, but honor the past."
—Peters

Journey Wall

DESCRIPTION/BACKGROUND

This is an extremely powerful activity for a group that has been around for a while. It enables new members to get on top of the history and background of the group very quickly. It also provides a tool for awakening the original vision and hopes that the long-time members brought to the inception of the group. In addition, this activity reminds the group of the historical and community events that provide the context for the group to have started in the first place.

Through this brainstorming of events in the world, the community, and the organization or group, people begin to see the kind of connections that foster the motivation of the group.

DID YOU KNOW?

- The big picture of why your company or organization grew out of happenings in the world around you can provide new appreciation for the role it plays.
- This activity can be the beginning of a powerful story about your company or organization.
- Seeing the chunks or phases of the organization's growth can assist the group in imagining the next phase.

ACTIVITY
#13 *Journey Wall*

1. Determine the years the group or organization has been around.

2. Across the top of a blank wall in front of the group, list the years it has been in existence. Use five- or ten-year increments if it has been around that long.

Examples:

1985 1986 1987 1988 1989 1990 1991 1992 1993 or

1945 1950 1955 1960 1965 1970 1975 1980 1985 1990 1993

3. On the same blank wall, down the left side, add these three major headings: World Events, Community or Local Events, Group or Organization Events.

4. Have individuals brainstorm events in all three categories since the group's inception. Give them three minutes for each category.

5. Have individuals write two or three best events for each category on 5 x 8 cards.

6. Then have them put the 5 x 8 cards on the wall, watching to make sure the cards are placed in the correct row and in the approximate year column.

7. When this is finished, there should be a wall with a large number of cards for each of the categories spread across the entire span of years.

8. The purpose of the following series of questions is to (1) help the group start absorbing the mass of information on the wall and (2) begin to discern the "chapters" of the story they are creating on the journey wall.

    a. Looking at the cards across the World Events row, which cards stand out for you?

    b. What relationships do you see among the World Events cards?

    c. Looking at the cards in the Community or Local Events row, which cards do you notice especially? What connections do you see among the events or happenings there?

    d. Looking at the Group or Organization Events cards, which cards were you glad to see up there? Which of these cards seem to flow together?

    e. Now looking across all the cards together, where do you see connections among the world, community, and organization events?

    f. Where would you make the three or four major breaks in this organization's history?

g. What title would you give to each of the three or four sections of this organization's history?

h. What title would you give to the whole history: The Great Story of _____ ?

9. You might try a processing question to end this activity, such as: What happened to your understanding of this organization as you participated in this Journey Wall?

Hints . . .

✓ **You can have different topics down the side. When working with a group of educators, you could substitute Events in the World of Education for Community or Local Events.**

✓ **I have used Events in the World of Education as the first row, Events in my Own Life for the second row, then the Group or Organization Events for the third row. The nature of the group and your task will provide you clues as to what categories to use.**

✓ **You can do additional things with this Journey Wall. You can ask people what kind of music they hear in each of the sections. You can ask people what colors or sounds go in each section. I have even been in a group that created a pantomime dance for each section of the story!**

EXAMPLE

THE GREAT STORY OF RESPONDING TO A PEOPLE'S NEEDS			
	Feeling Our Way	**Growing in Confidence**	**Expanding Our Service**
	1973–1977	1978–1982	1983–1987	1988–1993
WORLD EVENTS	Oil Embargo–OPEC Nixon Resigns U.S.A.–200th-year Bicentennial	Reagan and Thatcher Iranian Hostages AIDS	Expansion of Computers Corazon Aquino Elected in Philippines Ethiopian Famine Gorbachev	Berlin Wall Collapses Collapse of Soviet Union Gulf War
LOCAL EVENTS	Citywide Needs Survey Tornado Disaster	Major Industry Moves to Texas New City Cultural Center Influx of Asian Refugees	New Statewide Industry Campaign Flood Damage New Tax System	Current Mayor Elected Downtown Fire New Industry Relocates to Area
ORGANIZATION EVENTS	Organization Formed 10 Employees	4 More Locations Print Newsletter 2 Additional Departments	National Recognition Major Fund-Raising Campaigns First Statewide Conference	100 Employees Total Computerization International Liaisons

FOR THE COMMITTED

PURPOSEFUL VISION

#14

"Effective visions make sense in the marketplace, and, by stressing flexibility and execution, stand the test of time in a turbulent world." —Peters

Global Events Conversation

DESCRIPTION/BACKGROUND

You may not always have the amount of time necessary for the luxury of a Journey Wall. In that case, in ten to fifteen minutes you can still have a great impact with a global events conversation. This series of questions produces enough data and participation to help people see that whatever they are dealing with in their organization or community is related to things that are happening all over the world. Furthermore, at the very end when the question of positive trends is asked, people can discern that there are powerful historical and global forces working with us on behalf of our future.

DID YOU KNOW?

- Feeling connected to the whole world empowers people.
- Expanding your sense of belonging deepens your sense of responsibility.
- Linking yourself to the world alters your consciousness.

ACTIVITY

#14 *Global Events Conversation*

Below is the series of questions I use with a whole group. You are hoping for several responses to each question. Do not worry about a few seconds of silence as people collect their thoughts after you ask a question.

1. When I deal with a specific organization, I phrase the questions to focus in that area. For example: "What has been going on around the world and around the nation that has impacted the education community (or the health community, the world of finance)?"

2. Similarly, what has been going on around the state or local region that has impacted your organization?

3. How have you experienced this? In other words, what are the concrete manifestations of the impact of these events in your situation?

4. What creative and positive solutions to some of these issues have you read about, heard about, seen, or tried yourself?

5. As we do our planning today, what are some of the broad, positive trends we want to capitalize on in some way?

Hints . . .

✓ If participation seems to be a problem or if only one or two people are participating, you may want to do some of these questions in a round-robin fashion.

✓ Remember that you are not looking for a total, comprehensive list of responses. You want concrete answers so that once a flavor is achieved, you can then move on to the next question.

✓ With a very alert group, I have even added a final question to encourage their thinking about the reasons behind using this conversation: "Why have I started our workshop session today with this conversation?"

✓ The tricky thing about leading this kind of conversation is that this is not a time for speeches. You want a mosaic of responses. Consequently, when you begin to get long answers, repeat the question adding a little direction such as "in a phrase . . ." or "just mentioning the event. . . ." In addition, this conversation is not the time for debate or disagreements. In a sense you are building a verbal montage and then stepping back and talking about it. This conversation can happen very powerfully in just fifteen minutes.

✓ You might note if there are obvious gaps in the responses. If people have only given responses from the world and not mentioned anything nationally or vice versa, you can prompt people to think of some events from the area left out so far. Remember that your role is basically the leader. It is not necessary for you to contribute any responses at all.

EXAMPLE

When I met with a health care organization, they needed to get some perspective on the issues they were struggling with. The following global events conversation helped us set the tone for the day.

What has been going on around the world and nation that is affecting your business?
- Businesses moving out of the country
- Competition from other countries
- High cost of health care
- Deregulation
- Technological advances
- Environmental consciousness

What has been going on in the state or local region that is affecting your business?
- Rise in local taxes
- Companies have moved to other regions
- State regulations
- Company locations have shut down

How have you experienced this?
- Hard to find qualified employees
- Downsizing
- Low employee morale
- Employees must pay for part of their health insurance

What creative and positive solutions are you observing?
- Employees participating in appropriate management decisions
- Emphasis on employee retraining
- Streamlining of previously complex procedures
- Employee recognition programs

What are some of the broad positive trends we want to capitalize on?
- Rise of technology
- Increase in team-shared decision making
- Increasing global mobility
- Lowering of traditional East-West boundaries

For
The
Committed

**PURPOSEFUL
VISION**

"The origin of the vision is much less important than the process whereby it comes to be shared. It is not truly a 'shared vision' until it connects with the personal visions of people throughout the organization." —Senge

Newsletter

DESCRIPTION/BACKGROUND

Depending on the nature of the team, regular communication to an appropriate constituency might be helpful. Even something fairly simple could have a big impact. One sheet of paper every month, summarizing some key happenings, could go a long way. Making it imaginative and having it focus on just two or three things could do a lot to communicate what your team has done. This step is particularly useful when little communication is going on and there is a felt need for more.

Getting the word out about what you are doing increases motivation and commitment toward your work. This is one vehicle for sustaining the vision that brought the team or group together. The feedback generated from such communication is also extremely valuable.

DID YOU KNOW?

- A newsletter can signal "Wake up! Something is happening!"
- A newsletter keeps reminding people of the power in their own thinking and doing.
- Seeing things in print makes the items, the events, or the issues feel more real.

ACTIVITY

#15 *Newsletter*

Because a newsletter reminds the team that its vision is becoming a reality and that its efforts are making a difference, this activity cements the team, and adds to its sense of connection, a critical component of consensus.

1. If such a regular communication vehicle as a newsletter does not fit your particular situation, perhaps Activity #12, Article, will make more sense.

2. Meeting Products Documentation (Activity #8) is critical to providing regular material, some of which may be very appropriate for use in a newsletter.

3. If providing such a newsletter is a genuine team decision, then its implementation can also be a team effort. This is not meant to be one more burdensome task on the back of any one person or the leader.

4. A ten-minute brainstorm every so often can give enough grist for creating the content of each edition. Do this brainstorm on chart paper so that you can refer back to it.

5. Check in regularly with the team to see if the timing of the newsletter is still appropriate. If once a month seems too burdensome, how about once every six weeks? If the team is excited and if lots of mileage is coming back from the newsletter, maybe once every two or three weeks is better than once a month.

Hints . . .

✓ These days there are many desktop publishing programs and tools to fit either PCs or Apple Macintoshes. If your team decides a newsletter fits your situation, my general guideline for getting started is simplicity.

✓ One page done extremely well is better than four pages done poorly.

✓ The external function of this newsletter is getting the word out. The internal function can be just as critical—that of telling the story and keeping the vision alive and expanding.

EXAMPLE

A planning and implementation workshop, for business and education partnerships in a town in Wisconsin, initiated a joint effort called Partnership Projects. They initiated a very simple newsletter called Partnership Projects UPDATE. One month they featured articles entitled:

September (a review of what was to happen that month)

Invention Convention (a report on the carrying out of one of the projects planned for at the original planning workshop)

Job Shadowing (a report on another of the projects implemented out of the original planning workshop)

Our School District Adopts Business/School Partnership (a report of the adoption of this project as one of the School District's goals for the coming year)

Logo Development (a report of the development of a Partnership Project logo to be used on all further written communications)

"People need 'guiding stars' to navigate and make decisions day to day. But core values are only helpful if they can be translated into concrete behaviors."—Senge

FOR THE COMMITTED

PURPOSEFUL VISION

Organization Principles Workshop

DESCRIPTION/BACKGROUND

When a group has just recently come together or when you have a group that is very divided on a concern, discerning the total framework of principles can create a powerful ground of agreement and can enable real consensus.

When people put aside their anxieties about particular emotional concerns, they become surprised at the tremendous agreement they have on what they really want. By turning their attention to the valued principles they wish to hold in their solutions, they begin to see that perhaps they have some connections with this group after all; this is a group they can trust and with which they can negotiate and compromise.

DID YOU KNOW?

- Valued principles touch people more deeply than money.
- Valued principles give meaning to people's work.
- Consensus on principles taps a deep commitment in people.

ACTIVITY

#16 *Organization Principles Workshop*

1. Give a short context explaining why you are suggesting the group spend some time looking at their valued principles.

2. Have the group do some individual thinking for a few moments on what principles they want this organization to represent.

3. In groups of two or three, have them talk through what they feel are some of the most important principles.

4. Have them choose the five or six most critical ones and write them on 5 x 8 cards.

5. Once each mini-team has completed its cards, gradually call for the cards to be turned in. For example, have the groups pass up their most clear one first. See Activity #7 entitled Cardstorming.

6. As you place the cards on a wall with tape, ask the group to organize similar cards together.

7. When all the cards have been passed forward and several clusters have been created, have the group title each cluster.

8. This represents the whole framework of your group's valued principles.

9. Ask one or two processing questions on the valued principles: What surprised or pleased you about this picture of our principles? What does this reveal to us?

Hints . . .

✓ **Keep people focused on the subject of principles and not on their concerns for solutions.**

✓ **Although the group does not need to like every card on the wall, it is realistic to hope that the titles of the several clusters are principles the whole group is behind. This may give a group its first sense of authentic consensus.**

✓ **At this point you may be able to move the group to questions such as "What does this say about what we want our organization to look like concretely?" or "What specific directions or programs would hold these principles?" Or you may be able to proceed to a question of actions—"What concrete actions could bring about an organization with these principles?"**

✓ **Depending on the mood of the group, you might even be able to ask, "What happened to us as a group as we went through this workshop?" Again, you hope that people are starting to experience some genuine connection with each other or a sense of working as a team.**

EXAMPLE

When I began work on a very long-term, six-month process with a group, we asked this question: "What presuppositions, values, guidelines, and hopes do we have for this process of creating a solution that is based on consensus?"

They decided these were some of the values our process would hold:

> dynamic, open-minded process
> obstacles are opportunities
> collaborative teamwork
> climate of respect
> definite and positive results

PURPOSEFUL
VISION

"A vision statement is a document around which an organization can build its culture, as American culture is built around the Declaration of Independence and the Bill of Rights." —Richards, Engel, from Adams

Purposeful Vision Chart

DESCRIPTION/BACKGROUND

This activity creates a simple chart utilizing the cardstorming technique talked about in Activity #7. This full workshop draws individual hopes for the future of the organization into a total picture of what the group desires.

This picture is really the starting point for any serious planning or goal setting a group needs.

DID YOU KNOW?

- People take personal ownership in a product that represents their own thinking and effort.
- Seeing a group's vision in an organized chart can make it appear more realizable.
- Returning to such a chart a few months later helps to clearly see the areas that are already active as well as the areas that need more attention.

A C T I V I T Y

#17 *Purposeful Vision Chart*

1. After setting a context about why the work on vision is going on at this time, ask the group what concrete things they see happening in their organization a few years from now.

2. Give people individual time to jot down some answers.

3. In teams of two or three have people talk through their ideas.

4. Then have the teams write several responses on 5 x 8 cards in large letters, keeping their total words to three or four per card.

5. Ask each group to pass up one of their cards, perhaps the most clear.

6. Attach these cards to a front wall using masking tape loops.

7. Ask for more cards, perhaps the most different card from each team.

8. As you attach these to the front wall, ask the group to note cards that are connected to each other.

9. Move those cards together so that gradually clusters are formed.

10. After attaching some temporary titles to the clusters, assign a number, letter, or symbol to each cluster.

11. Ask the groups to assign the appropriate number, letter, or symbol to their remaining cards if those cards naturally gravitate toward one of the clusters.

12. Call for the rest of the cards to come forward.

13. Talk through the cards not yet clustered to see where they belong.

14. After placing all the cards into clusters, proceed to polish the temporary titles of the clusters to specific statements of what that column is representing in their vision.

15. As a processing question, I often ask individuals to name which cluster particularly interests or excites them.

16. Be sure that someone types this product into a chart that will be available for the next meeting.

Hints . . .

✓ **Read Activity #7 on cardstorming first.**

✓ **When you are working with any group on planning, it is always important to begin with where you want to go and not begin with the problems or obstacles you are already facing. To do so sets a negative tone to your work right from the start.**

✓ **After getting the noun the cluster is about, then ask the group for two or three adjectives to clarify precisely what is wanted for that cluster.**

✓ **Be sure to allow up to an hour to accomplish this activity.**

EXAMPLE

In working with a group from a bank concerned about improving customer service, the following chart represented their three-year purposeful vision.

NORTHTOWN NATIONAL BANK The 3-Year Practical Vision				
Improved Customer Services		Profitable Growth and Expansion	Expanded Training and Equipment	
Customer Convenience Services	Customer-Oriented Organizational Efficiency		Individualized Customer Service Training	Advanced Time-Saving Equipment
More Advanced Teller Terminal	Bulk Filing to Save Time	Broader Market Base	Courteous, Prompt, Efficient Service	More Computers and PCs
Call in Your Check Order on Voice Mail	Less Turnover of Staff	More Flexibility in Jobs	Better Equipped to Service More Sophisticated Clients	More Modern Phone System
ATMs	Better Networking	Expand to One More Facility		Automatic Statement Copier
		Concierge in Lobby	Have Salaries Increased	
Automatic Coin Counters in Lobby	Customer Input	Broader Advertising	Better Communication with Other Departments	More Advanced CRT Terminals

PARTICIPATIVE PROCESSES

"Besides demographic differences, today's workforce holds a new set of values which are quite different from those of previous generations. The Protestant Work Ethic has been replaced by the notion that work should be fun, or at least personally satisfying." (Spencer, 1989, p. 6)

A new sense of work values the participation of every individual in the creation of organizational directions. There is a growing sense that human resources are perhaps the most valuable asset an organization has. In addition, organizations are discovering that utilizing not only a person's hands but also a person's head and commitment can enhance total effectiveness. More succinctly, ignoring an individual's passion and concern is ignoring a huge resource. Only with participation and consensus can that passion be tapped for the sake of the work of the organization.

What are called for are ways to tap the wisdom and creativity of the entire staff. The issues are too huge and complex to permit responses and solutions to come from a handful when there are huge mental resources and energy to tap in the entire staff. This calls for letting people know the crucial data necessary to make informed decisions. This means trusting people with information that until now was often reserved for just a few.

One way to do that is to create connections between individual aims and whole organizational goals. In other words, the process of genuine consensus starts from individual desires and hopes and moves to building whole organizational strategies and directions. When this step occurs well, deep personal energy is tapped for carrying out the work of the organization.

Consensus is the link between effective participation and committed action. The crucial link between full participation and committed action is an experience of consensus which provides a focus and a direction to the participation. A brainstormed list of ideas is a fine first step. But moving beyond a mere list to sensing what the list is telling is absolutely crucial.

In other words, participation alone is not enough. People want to see that their participation is going somewhere and is making a difference. People want to see a connection between their ideas and what actually occurs in the life of the organization. The only way to move from authentic participation to committed action is through genuine consensus. Participation leads to ownership only when there has been consensus; that is, when there has been a sense of the individual pieces coming together to form some kind of organized whole.

Spencer suggests that underneath the despair and cynicism that many people are manifesting today is a deep desire to pour their energies into something that will work. While people want to make this kind of commitment, they want to participate in what they will be committed to. If they desire to be committed to something larger than themselves, they want to see some piece of themselves in that larger thing.

Genuine participation itself is complex. It is part of a whole, growing, and directed process. Participation is part of the big picture of directing and leading an organization. Participation is not something you do just once and it is not something that can be turned on at the whim of some leader or group of leaders. Participation is an ongoing mode of operating that requires new sets of skills in order to initiate and sustain.

Now add to this the fact that today, beyond the dynamic of participation, there is further complexity. The staff of any organization is more diverse than ever before. Often it is multi-racial, multi-ethnic, multi-religious, and multi-age. Furthermore, many problematic issues are often not just located within the organization itself but may be endemic in the entire society. All this is to say that creating consensus in the midst of this kind of complexity and diversity is more difficult than perhaps ever before in our society.

Although this may look like an overwhelming burden impossible to resolve, it also points us in the direction of the solution. The diversity we meet in the workplace is precisely our asset for solutions. With appropriate skills, we can use that diversity to create solutions that are born of consensus. The wealth in perspective and creativity can assist in solving the concerns and issues we face.

Managers, leaders, and principals who attempt to keep their hands in everything will soon discover it is totally impossible. They can only head toward burnout or more participative, consensus-generating modes. The reason for this is simple: no one person can be expected to have all the answers today. The issues we face are overwhelmingly complex. The world, contemporary technology, and our ever-changing society have emerged into a complexity that only a multitude of minds and perspectives can possibly succeed in uncovering workable solutions.

"However, even the desire to participate or to have participation is not enough. Participation involves team members acquiring a new set of skills" (Blake et al., 1987, p. 127). Because of the increasing complexity, consensus requires learning new skills appropriate to the more participative and facilitative environment of today's workplace.

Gradually as these skills are utilized, people will become more and more comfortable and confident with them. The very use of these skills often pits those attempting to use them against a conscious or unconscious hostile environment. Many times I have been asked to facilitate participative planning only to discover that the leader who asked me had no actual desire to empower his or her staff or employees at all. It is as if the leader wanted wisdom only on behalf of continuing top-down leadership.

Consensus refers to lateral connections. Powerful lateral connections are rightfully a threat to strong top-down hierarchies. And so this adds even more dimensions to the complexity of genuine consensus. Likewise, powerful lateral connections are precisely what enhance the possibility of consensus.

**PARTICIPATIVE
PROCESSES**

GENERATING TOTAL PARTICIPATION

INTRODUCTION TO PARTICIPATION

Genuine participation is difficult to achieve. It is easy to criticize the early efforts to create authentic participation. It is also easy to note the faults in some of the early products. Trusting that full participation is absolutely vital to whatever goal a leader might have does not come naturally. It is easy, on the other hand, to fall back on tried and true top-down approaches. Sometimes this happens very subtly. Many well-intentioned leaders begin, "Now I want everyone to participate in reaching this decision." Then these same leaders proceed to talk nonstop for thirty minutes. Participation is blocked from the start. Other leaders allow a few comments but soon they jump in sensing a need to defend a position, comment, or action.

Many times, leadership just does not have the tools to release genuine participation. More often than not, people either fear such participation or do not really trust that full participation can achieve powerful results.

On the other hand, people are in no mood to consider consensus if they feel their voice is never heard. The truth is that some people are willing to move toward consensus and trust the group with just knowing the group has heard their point of view—even if the final position has modified and altered their original suggestion.

Unguided participation does not in itself breed trust or automatically move a group toward consensus. Furthermore, people's relationship to participation sours if some tangible result is not evident. People will only depart from the old authoritarian ways if some care is given to the focus and direction of participation.

People yearn to feel that their insights are welcomed and even trusted by their leaders. When this trust is genuine, participation is enhanced and great human resources are properly channeled into actions and solutions.

Simple
Things
To
Do

**PARTICIPATIVE
PROCESSES**

"Participation in decision-making offers employees valued opportunities to align personal goals with those of their companies and enhances the meaningful nature of their work." —Spencer

Creating the Real Question

DESCRIPTION/BACKGROUND

In this activity, people write down what they think the critical question is for the particular meeting to address. Then the leader pulls several of these together, guiding the group in creating the *one* question the meeting will address.

This not only creates some early participation, but it also provides a focus for the rest of the meeting. In addition, it gives the alert leader some critical information about what is on people's minds. Referrals back to these individual questions later on in the meeting will give the group confidence that the leader has paid attention to what was said.

DID YOU KNOW?

- Helping a group figure out the real question gives the group its first experience of consensus.
- Coming up with the one question for a session provides a clean focus for the meeting.
- You can remind the group of this question if you think the meeting is getting off track.

ACTIVITY

#18 *Creating the Real Question*

1. Open the meeting in an appropriate way, such as by introducing your-self.

2. Present this statement to the group: "I would like each of you to think a moment and then write down the *one* question you sense we need to address today."

3. Prepare chart paper in the front of the room.

4. After people have a chance to think and write, ask for some volunteers to share their questions.

5. Write all the questions on chart paper in the front of the room, even if some seem repetitive.

6. When five or six questions have been shared, ask the group, "Where do you see some similarities or commonalities?"

7. Gradually work with the group to build the real question by asking, "What do you think is the one question this meeting is out to address?"

8. Indicate to the group that at the end of the meeting the question will be checked to make sure the meeting has dealt with it.

9. Then at the end of the meeting, ask the group, "How has this meeting dealt with the real question?"

Hints . . .

✓ This ten-minute exercise has the potential of not only generating participation but on a very foundational level creating an early experience of consensus. It can generate a mood of accomplishment very early in a meeting.

✓ Keep the question posted up front. It will indirectly keep people focused on the top priority of that meeting.

✓ A variation of this might be used after you have created or presented a long agenda. You might ask the group to prioritize the agenda.

EXAMPLE

Recently, I went to a school to lead a two-hour session on goal setting. It was not possible for me to meet with any of the staff ahead of time. About the only thing I knew beforehand was the topic, Goal Setting. As I saw it, there were several possible slants to this: How do I help my students set class goals? How do I help my students set their own personal goals? How do I better set goals for my own teaching?

After the introduction, I asked, "As you have thought about this session today, what is the one question you hoped to get some help on?" After jotting down their own individual responses, several people shared their questions:

How do I get goals accomplished in the class with so many interruptions?

What do I do when my goals fall apart in a couple of months? Is it O.K. to readjust my goals?

How do you carry out goals when the students' academic levels are so divergent?

After writing all these responses on chart paper in the front, I moved to a blank sheet saying, "Looking at these questions, what seem to be some common elements to them?" Gradually the group created one question: "How can I increase my ability to get my goals accomplished for the students in the classroom?"

Simple
Things
To
Do
PARTICIPATIVE PROCESSES

"Meetings sparked with humorous stories, celebrations of individual or corporate milestones, brief relaxation or energizing exercises or special refreshments at strategic intervals are eventful and enlivening."
—Spencer

Eventful Happenings

DESCRIPTION/BACKGROUND

There are gifted people who can take an ordinary meeting, add pizzazz, and make an event out of it. It is easy around holidays to do something special to a meeting. It is even easier to celebrate a birthday and add something extra to a humdrum meeting. There are many things you can do to liven up a meeting to help motivate your team and keep it going.

Eventful happenings create the mood of excitement and anticipation that relaxes people. They bond the group. They can set the stage for genuine consensus. They remind us that our colleagues in this group are great and significant human beings. When you believe that about your colleagues, you discover you might want to come to consensus with them.

DID YOU KNOW?

- Events motivate us and call forth participation from us.
- Positive events are a way of taking care of team members.
- Eventful meetings create an anticipation for the next meeting.

ACTIVITY

#19 *Eventful Happenings*

This activity really suggests that you spend time every so often stepping back and thinking about where your group is and what it needs next.

1. Find ways to read the mood of your group frequently.

   a. In processing questions, ask people what the mood of the group is.

   b. Note people's expressions when they arrive and when they leave. People have arrived at my meetings after long days at work, looking completely wiped out. I watch them come back to life and become energized.

   c. Pay attention to the kinds of things that are talked about, the tone of people's voices, and the animation in their facial expressions.

2. When you see that meetings have lost their original excitement and anticipation, it is time to act by bringing something different to the meeting.

3. Is it time to:
   - Go to lunch together?
   - Celebrate a recent victory?
   - Recognize everyone in the group with something simple?
   - Sit back and recount the recent accomplishments?
   - Invite the managers in to say a few words of praise?
   - Write up what this group has been doing and get it into the papers or reported somewhere?
   - See a movie together?

All of these are ways to transform the ordinary into something special.

Hints . . .

✓ If you are the type who does not feel very imaginative, more than likely someone with flair in your group would be delighted to liven things up a bit at the next meeting. Maybe you could name that person with a special title and rotate that title to a different person for each meeting.

✓ Whatever is done can communicate to people that their participation is special and valued. You can get a lot of energy and participation from people when they believe this about themselves.

EXAMPLE

A group I worked with wanted to get community people and parents to attend a Saturday morning meeting to brainstorm some possible solutions to the issue of overcrowding at their school. One teacher came up with the idea to create a play of several short vignettes dramatizing the overcrowding issue. Twenty-five to thirty students would all have parts in these vignettes. In various scenes, these students portrayed a special education class that had to meet in the hall, seventh and eighth graders that ate lunch in the auditorium instead of the cafeteria, and first and second graders that feared to walk up flights of stairs crowded with bigger seventh and eighth grade students. All of this clarified the issue and made it come alive. It was a dynamic event that increased attendance dramatically at this voluntary Saturday morning public meeting. Two hundred people were in the auditorium to watch the play, and seventy-five actually stayed for the full morning of workshops.

"The concept of employee partici-pation has taken hold so firmly that it is hard to find a current book about management that doesn't either promote participa-tion or assume it." —Spencer

Sticker Dots

DESCRIPTION/BACKGROUND

The Sticker Dots activity quickly reveals the mind of a group while getting everyone into the act. Members of the group place one or more dots on various items as a way for all to see what the mind of the whole group is. When all the dots have been placed, a conversa-tion can help to process the picture the group has just created.

Objective ways of showing the mind of a group to itself are necessary. In other words, one important step in building consensus is to help a group see its own thinking. Sticker dots is one way to do this. With the flurry of activity and drama, people can hardly argue with the picture that is created. It may not agree with their own thinking, but no one can question that it represents the mind of the group.

Once this picture is created, you can then begin to dialogue with the ideas represented in the picture and not with any particular personalities in the group. This helps people get one step away from their emotions and one step closer to consensus.

DID YOU KNOW?

- In the Sticker Dots activity you involve everyone in creating an art form.
- This activity is great in multilingual situations.

A C T I V I T Y

#20 *Sticker Dots*

1. Gather the materials beforehand: sticker dots (several colors if you decide to go that way), chart paper to write the various directions or ideas on, container or containers for the dots.

2. Prepare chart paper ahead of time listing the various items you want the group to evaluate.

3. Decide whether people will get just one dot apiece or three colors with a different value for each color (e.g., a blue dot is worth three points, a red dot is worth two points, and a green dot is worth one point).

4. Prepare a brief context about the issues or the steps the group has taken to get this far. Clearly indicate the precise question or issue the dot activity is about.

5. Pass out the dots.

6. Invite all team members to come forward and place their dots onto their choices of the items listed on the chart paper.

7. Indicate that they may put one, two, or three of their dots on one choice if they feel that strongly about it.

8. Choose a couple of the following questions to help the group process what the picture is telling them:

   a. What do you notice?

   b. What surprises you?

   c. What interests you?

   d. How does this picture demonstrate the group's thinking about the issues before us?

   e. What are the implications of this picture?

   f. What are our next steps?

Hints . . .

✓ You can use this activity at a public meeting to get a reading of even a large group's mind about something.

✓ If the attendance is more than sixty people, you may want to prepare two such lists and place them in different parts of the room to avoid a logjam when you call people to come forward to place their dots.

✓ If you are doing this with such a large group, probably one dot per person will be adequate.

✓ Be sure to have a recorder tally the dots so that a report can be passed out to the group at the next meeting.

EXAMPLE

Working with a committee of a local school council in Chicago, it came time to present a variety of recommendations to the council and others attending the council meeting. The principal and committee chair each gave a short context on the issue and the process we were using to arrive at our recommendations. At that point, I stood up and reviewed the recommendations. I then gave directions for how they were to use the sticker dots.

"When you come up to the list, you will find three bowls of different-colored dots. The blue dots are worth three points, red dots two points, and green dots one point. Each person can place one dot of each color anywhere on the list. You can even put more than one dot on one item."

People came forward. There was a lot of buzzing and energy flowing as people put their dots onto the list. It took about five minutes for forty people to place their dots.

After they finished I asked, "What does the picture of dots tell us about our thinking on these recommendations?" They easily noticed where most of the dots lay and where they did not fall. It was hard to argue about what the mind of the group was.

Simple
Things
To
Do

**PARTICIPATIVE
PROCESSES**

*"Workers also want to be treated
with respect. Rather than mere
order-takers, most valuable
employees consider themselves to
be as intelligent as their superiors
and they want that intelligence to
be recognized." —Spencer*

Language

DESCRIPTION/BACKGROUND

Language has the potential of inviting or closing off participation.
Particular words and phrases can actually enhance the atmosphere
of participation. Not only guidelines such as asking questions more
than making pronouncements (see Activity #23, Questions Not
Dictums), but the vocabulary and style of the language can also
increase participation.

Language is powerful. It is also second nature to us. It is easy to
be unaware of what our language does to the people around us.
Especially if we are in a stated leadership position, we may not
always get the kind of feedback about what we say and the impact it
has.

DID YOU KNOW?

- Language can either invite and beckon or turn people away.
- Language includes both the words and the tone—either one can turn people
  off or call for their participation.
- Some people actually write out a script ahead of time to guard the use of
  their words and tone.

A C T I V I T Y

#21 *Language*

The Less Helpful column includes comments which I believe cut off participation or cause people to hesitate before saying something. The More Helpful column includes alternative ways of communicating what is in the Less Helpful column.

LESS HELPFUL	MORE HELPFUL
That's a weird idea.	Could you clarify that for us? Say a little more about that.
We spent all last year resolving that.	What do you think is still unclear about that?
I don't see what that has to do with the question.	Please help me see the connection between what you've just said and our main question now.
Should we increase the support staff?	What are some things we could do to solve this issue?
Shall we cut the materials budget?	What are some steps we could take to solve this money crunch?
What do you think of my list of criteria for the new staff person?	What would be helpful qualifications to look for in our new staff person?
You've left something out.	I like your next focus on cost-cutting procedures.

Note: There are a lot of questions in the More Helpful column because often, well-stated questions encourage participation more than statements.

Hints . . .

✓ If you are courageous, you might tape record yourself at a typical meeting. When you play it back, listen for comments or things said that seemed to occasion responses. Then pay attention to things you said that brought a lot of silence. Try to figure out what made the difference. It may have just happened that way— or it may have had something to do with what you said or how you said it. Note the tone of your voice. Does it invite participation?

✓ If you have been in a leadership position for a long time, much of what you do and say is by now very natural. You might try scripting out your next meeting. Write down exactly what you are going to say. Note your questions. If you are giving instructions, pay attention to how you give them.

✓ Are you genuinely inviting participation or are you really asking for a rubber stamp on what you have already decided?

EXAMPLE

One week I worked with a different group each day on a planning workshop. In one group, I noticed that whenever the leader made a comment it was to affirm what someone had just said or to make a very appropriate positive and encouraging suggestion. "We could do this idea at the same time we are doing this event." or "It would be possible for us to adjust our schedule in this way."

The following day I was in a group whose leader from time to time would get me aside and say, "What's the matter with these people? Why aren't they thinking about X? Why haven't they generated more data about Y?" I suggested he introduce his concerns in a manner conducive to group empowerment such as by asking, "Have you considered X?" or "When does Y fit into your total plan?"

#22

"Participation is perhaps the surest way to inspire commitment. Participation in planning and decision-making leads to ownership, and that in turn builds the commitment that is a prerequisite for excellence in workmanship." —Spencer

TV News Spot

DESCRIPTION/BACKGROUND

In order to give people a feel for pulling off an event, to help bridge gaps among team members, and to call forth a different level of participation from team members, I ask them to choose one of the activities that is already in their plan and to create a three-minute TV news spot reporting on its successful completion. After the presentations, I ask a couple of processing questions to help them think through what has just happened.

Spontaneous creativity using both the left and right brain can call forth unique skills and talents that are normally not present in a typical meeting. (The left brain is considered to be the more logical and rational part; the right brain, the more creative and intuitive.) During the presentations by small teams, incredible appreciation is generated for the creativity and talents of everyone involved. This activity lays a foundation for appreciation of others' ideas and appreciation for the opportunity of full participation. Because of its potential for creating connections among people, it is a tool for creating consensus down the road.

DID YOU KNOW?

- An opportunity for creativity not only calls forth participation but provides a moment of bonding and connecting.
- Standing in the "victory circle" builds momentum and confidence to complete the project.
- In doing this activity others can become as excited with your project as you are.

ACTIVITY

#22 *TV News Spot*

1. Use the teams or the mini-teams that are already part of your group.

2. After they have done some planning on the activities they are going to do during the coming year, have each team choose one activity or planned event.

3. Suggest they create a three-minute TV news spot to report on the occurrence of the event or the successful completion of the project.

4. Give everyone ten minutes to create their news spot.

5. Have each team give its presentation.

6. Applaud and recognize the efforts of each team after its presentation.

7. Allow time for one or two processing questions:

    a. How did your team work together?

    b. What did you learn?

    c. What really happened during this news spot exercise?

Hints . . .

✓ You might have a few creative materials such as colored paper, scissors, glue, cards, and markers available for people to use in creating props.

✓ There are many beneficial results from this simple strategy. First, dramatizing the power of events and happenings indirectly suggests to the team that events and clear-cut accomplishments create excitement and motivation, not long drawn-out committees or projects that take years and years.

✓ One of the other impacts of this activity is the breaking down of barriers among team members. People get to look at each other in a new light as they watch each other create this news spot.

EXAMPLE

Leading a conference for business people and local educators, I decided to insert this activity just before they did some serious planning. They had already laid out several possible highly motivating events. Each team had a mix of teachers and business people.

The presentations were humorous and informative, representing a real belief that something important could be created. Creativity ran rampant. Someone found a mop in the hotel to use as a microphone. Many "hams" had a chance to shine.

During the processing conversation, I asked what happened. Many business people said, "I had no idea how professional our teachers are. They really know about teaching." Likewise, the teachers said, "We had no idea how much these business people care about the future of our community and our children." Barriers were broken down in a short amount of time.

#23

"It can be taken for granted that most organization members want to participate as fully and productively as possible, and that something blocks this happening."
—Blake, Mouton, and Allen

Questions Not Dictums

DESCRIPTION/BACKGROUND

Open-ended questions are critical to generating the total participation of the group. A question that genuinely calls for true responses is one of the foundations to initiating participation. The phrasing of the question makes a difference. "What do you think about the proposed solution?" is not as helpful as "What are some possible solutions to this issue?" The effective leader's time is often better spent devising the most accurate and inviting questions rather than worrying about the answers needed.

Although many meetings consist of hearing reports from various teams and offering suggestions or comments on these reports, other meetings are to discuss an issue or come up with some solutions to concerns. This is the kind of situation that can benefit from some real participation. It is at this point that the right question is crucial. The right question defines the concern but does not predict the "right" solution in its phrasing.

DID YOU KNOW?

- Like it or not, few people today want to be told exactly what to do.
- Questions invite; dictums turn people off.
- Questions communicate that you need help.
- Questions convey the truth—you do not have all the answers.

ACTIVITY

#**23**   *Questions Not Dictums*

1. Write down all the concerns and issues for your next meeting.

2. Sort through these and choose only the ones that must be dealt with at this meeting.

3. Your skill as a leader is discerning what really has to be worked on in your meeting.

4. Get clarity on the real issue and the meeting product that will most help you relative to this issue.

5. Use this thinking to help you frame the open-ended question that really invites answers from the group.

6. Think through how you want the answers to be given. Is this an informal conversation? Will a brainstorm list be helpful? Is this the kind of question that calls for a full workshop, using the 5 x 8 cards referred to in Activity #7? The advantage to cards is that they allow you to work with the responses, cluster them, and group them so that you can begin to see the similarity in the responses to your question.

7. Again, be sure to allow time for processing using one or two of these questions:

   a. What was helpful about our time together?

   b. What questions still remain for us?

   c. What are the next steps we need to take?

Hints . . .

✓ During the brainstorm process, your role is affirmation. Every answer has merit and helps the group come to a solution. As a leader, your imagination is called on at all times to see the gift in the responses offered.

✓ Needless to say, while you are leading, it may not appear that every answer is worthwhile. But to foster the process and to keep the ball rolling in people's minds, ongoing affirmation is crucial. Continually discerning the group wisdom rather than responding negatively to what seems like an off-the-wall response takes a great deal of discipline. Possibly responding here with, "John, say a little more about that," can reveal some hidden good idea.

✓ If several answers in a row seem off target, the whole group may still be unclear about the intent of the question. When this happens, gently repeat or rephrase the question. Usually that is enough to generate some on-target responses.

EXAMPLE

The Dictum column gives you examples of some dictums which undermine participation. The Question column illustrates questions that invite dialogue and creative thinking.

DICTUM	QUESTION
Tell me how you like this plan I've prepared.	What are some elements of a plan that will work for us?
This is how I want you to get this project done.	This is what we need accomplished. How might we get this done?
This is the way it's always been done.	Who has some ideas on more effective ways to get this done?
You've got to find ways to cut the cost of this.	What are some ways you've thought of to cut the cost of this?

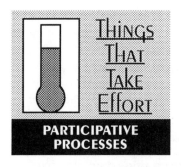

PARTICIPATIVE PROCESSES

ORGANIZING THE MEETING FOCUS

INTRODUCTION TO FOCUS

Many meetings fall flat on their face today because the organizer has not done the preparation and homework ahead of time to guarantee an effective and time-efficient meeting. If a one-hour meeting is scheduled, then one hour's worth of business needs to be planned. Many times we insert five hours worth of agenda into a one-hour meeting. This sets the meeting up for failure at the outset. Conversely, we may expect the meeting to run itself or just happen and consequently plan nothing. Meeting focus means clarity on the exact work to be accomplished, that is, clarity on the realistic products that can be expected from the amount of time scheduled.

There can be no clear idea of what participative processes you may want to use until you are clear about what you want the meeting to accomplish. Many unfocused meetings joined with haphazard participative processes have given participative processes a bad name.

When this occurs, distrust for the effectiveness of team collaboration grows. Consequently, trust in consensus diminishes. The leader then resorts to tried and true methods for making decisions and getting the job done. The organizer blames the team when in actuality the organizer's own poor meeting coordination is at fault. A clear focus that promises meeting accomplishments and enables them to happen is more critical than people realize in creating an atmosphere where consensus can grow confidently.

If the meeting agenda continually seems overwhelming and overcrowded, it is possible that you need to break the group down into smaller teams to bring recommendations for the agenda items. This would cut down the time for a whole group discussion that could be done by just two or three people, saving larger group discussion for concrete recommendations.

The activities in this section are all activities you as the leader can think about to help you organize a more effective meeting.

THiNGS
THAT
TAKE
EffORT
**PARTICIPATIVE
PROCESSES**

"The guiding principle here is to facilitate higher levels of performance, to empower others to act on their best intuition and skills." —Ackerman from Adams

One Concrete Product

DESCRIPTION/BACKGROUND

The organizer decides beforehand what concrete products are going to come out of the meeting. This could be a major decision about a current concern, a list of possible options relative to a major decision, an update on what is happening, or the responses to a particularly controversial situation. The organizer thinks through what the team can reasonably expect to accomplish in the time available. The push of this activity is that there be at least one visible, concrete product that people immediately recognize as the goal of the meeting. Meetings that go on and on with no visible product bring morale down quickly. Likewise, meetings with ten major concrete product goals paralyze those attending.

Bad meetings do not just happen. Their planners have usually ignored critical guidelines. Just because you encourage meetings with a participative process does not mean your job as the organizer or planner is finished. Choosing exactly what needs to come out of the meeting and mapping out the most helpful participative process to get your team there are tasks requiring leadership skill.

DID YOU KNOW?

- Two short, well-organized meetings might be more efficient than one long meeting.
- If your team is made up of eight people and you meet for one hour, you are using the resource of eight person hours.
- Meetings without any visible products drive people crazy.

ACTIVITY

#**24**   *One Concrete Product*

This activity is one you do yourself before the meeting.

1. List all the items that come to mind for the agenda.

2. Ask others on the team before the meeting for concerns or items they may have for the agenda.

3. Screen these items by asking yourself these questions:

   a. Which of these absolutely must get dealt with at this meeting?

   b. Which of these need some more small-team work to be ready for a fruitful team discussion?

   c. If we did put this on the agenda, what is the expected result of the whole team looking at it?

   d. Is this an item a subteam needs to talk through, returning to the next meeting with a set of recommendations?

   e. Is this an item that belongs with our team?

   f. If this issue is complicated, what piece of its resolution can be realistically handled at this meeting?

4. Separate your items into: Quick Items, Major Items, and Minor Items.

5. Put two or three of the Quick Items at the beginning of the agenda. Coming to rapid decisions at the front end of the meeting will provide some motivation for the team.

6. While the team is still fresh, choose to deal with the Major Items. Keeping to the time flow is critical here.

7. Wrapping up the meeting with some work on Minor Items should go fairly easily since the team will have already dealt with the most difficult items.

Hints . . .

✓ The skill here is determining what actually has to occur at this meeting. Certain agenda items can be accomplished outside the regular meeting. Other agenda items need some work before they are fully ready for the meeting.

✓ Knowing exactly what product you need relative to each minor action is just as critical as the major action.

✓ Most meetings restrict themselves to one major product. You will lose effectiveness if a group has to wrestle through and negotiate one difficult issue after another. You lose efficiency if you are always asking the whole group to hash through everything from start to finish without using small groups to do much of the hashing through before the meeting even begins.

✓ Watching the dynamics is important. If a resolution does not emerge, is something more needed? Are people worn out? Is there another time the final decision could be made? Is it time to point out what pieces have been resolved as a way to move people toward a resolution? Has enough discussion taken place that two or three people could be set aside for ten to fifteen minutes to bring their recommendation back to the table, while some of the minor items can be worked on? As a facilitator, you have many options for how to progress.

✓ The most debilitating thing about meetings is the sense that time is being wasted. A frequent comment is, "We spent all this time and did not accomplish a thing." Generally, people do not begrudge time itself, but they do begrudge wasted time.

EXAMPLE

Here is a sample of the kinds of meeting agenda items which might fall into each of the three categories.

QUICK ITEMS	MAJOR ITEMS	MINOR ITEMS
Team Reports from the Previous Week	Major Policy Decisions	Revamping Project Timeline
Information Updates	Creating a 6-month Plan	Shifts in Task Responsibilities
Reports on Shifts in Company Policy	Important Budget Revisions	Choosing Project Dates

THiNGs
THaT
Take
EffoRt

**PARTICIPATIVE
PROCESSES**

*"Conventional wisdom suggests
that effectiveness comes from a
strong leader, a clear mission, and
technically competent subordi-
nates. Yet more is involved if a
team is to realize synergy. The key
issue is in how the parts act
together—participation."* —Blake,
Mouton, and Allen

Time Flow Picture

DESCRIPTION/BACKGROUND

A Time Flow Picture is simply a visual layout of the meeting. I
recommend that before the meeting starts, the facilitator lay out the
flow of the meeting in a simple visual image to be presented at the
very beginning of the meeting.

Many leaders often prepare a list of the agenda items and pass
this out ahead of time. This is very helpful in that it demonstrates
some thinking about what needs to happen at the meeting. Often,
however, an agenda list gives no sense of priority, nor does it suggest
the actual flow of time.

An agenda list of twenty items for a designated meeting time of
ninety minutes communicates immediately no intention of making
the ninety-minute time frame. Morale immediately diminishes.
People need to believe that it is possible to accomplish the agenda
within the stated time frame. A time flow chart can communicate
that agenda goals are within reach.

DID YOU KNOW?

- Because people feel so pressed about time and schedules today, anxieties
  are reduced when people see a clear picture of the time flow.

- Some people today feel time is a more precious commodity than money.

- Since everyone has the same amount of time—168 hours every week—our
  only question is how best to use the time we are given.

ACTIVITY

#25 *Time Flow Picture*

1. Write down all of the components and elements of your meeting.

2. Make an initial layout of the flow from beginning to end (see Activity #24, One Concrete Product, for one way to do it.)

3. Lay the components of the meeting across your timeline so that you can see both the order and the time allotment for each item.

4. Check for feasibility.

5. Make a visual representation of your proposed time flow to present to your team at your next meeting.

MEETING FLOW		
Intro. 2 min.		
Quick Items	**Major Items**	**Minor Items**
10 min.	30 min.	16 min.
Concl. 2 min.		

Hints . . .

✓ Try to be honest about exactly how long each component will take to accomplish. That will help you to create a time flow picture that is truly realistic.

✓ I use small Post-it notes to lay out the elements I want to cover in the meeting. Then I rearrange them on my desk until I get the flow that makes sense to me.

✓ It is often difficult to start when only four of your ten team members have arrived on time. How can you proceed if only 40% of your team is there? Although there are times when it is necessary to wait, waiting teaches the 40% to come late next time, initiating a trend toward starting later and later. When I plan a meeting, I start with a conversation or a short activity to set the stage. It is usually quite enjoyable, but perhaps not crucial to the content of the whole meeting. This lets me start the meeting on time and still allow for some people to arrive late.

EXAMPLE

I was once in charge of training a group of people in complex finance procedures for a major project. My sessions typically looked like the following:

TRAINING SESSION FLOW		
Intro.	Where we are on project timeline— THE BIG PICTURE	**2 min.**
Quick Items	**Major Items**	**Minor Items**
Review and Polishing Last Meeting's Major Product	Training Session on Next Phase of Finance Procedures	Content of Team Report to Department Meeting Minor Task Realignments
12 min.	**25 min.**	**15 min.**
Concl.	Processing Question—What worked well for us in today's session?	**3 min.**

#26

Things
That
Take
Effort

PARTICIPATIVE
PROCESSES

"The effective, or ineffective, use of space at a meeting locale can exert a subtle yet powerful influence on the mood of participants and the ability of the group to focus its attention on the issues." —Spencer

Meeting Space

DESCRIPTION/BACKGROUND

The physical layout of meeting space is more important than we often realize. How you place the tables and chairs can communicate a great deal to the participants of the meeting. It is crucial to know ahead of time what the space looks like so that you can arrange it to best foster the participation of your team.

Some space, such as most board of education or town council meeting rooms, have the board or council seats on a raised dais, separating them from the public. They have tables and the public does not. This communicates that only the board or council is to make any significant impact on decisions. Theater-style room arrangements have everyone facing the platform or stage. Again, this communicates that all the action and decision making are up front. A room full of tables and chairs communicates that everyone is a participant. Although a room needs a focus (such as the front), it also needs a way for interaction to occur. Combining both of these can be tricky.

DID YOU KNOW?

- Neat table and chair arrangement communicates this meeting has a plan.
- Too many extra chairs around the table lowers the mood because it communicates that you expected many more people.

ACTIVITY

#26 *Meeting Space*

Here are things to review as you plan the layout of your meeting space.

1. Decide the best working wall for the meeting (i.e., where the chart paper or 5 x 8 cards are going to go up).

2. Arrange the tables so that people sitting at both the long sides can see the front. Or, if people are not going to spend much time in separate teams or subgroups, tables can be connected (as shown below).

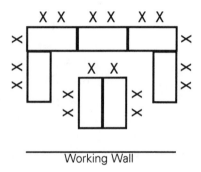

Working Wall

3. If you are intending for work in teams to take up a lot of meeting time, arrange your tables into separate team tables as shown.

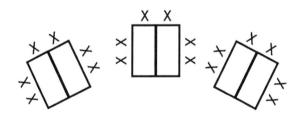

Working Wall

Hints . . .

✓ Unless you are very spatially gifted, there is no substitute for showing up early to the meeting space and checking it out. Very often even a little rearrangement can make a difference.

✓ I often discover that while most people want to set up a meeting to face the obvious front, creating the focus along a side wall gives more wall work space and allows more people to be closer to the working wall.

✓ Since the focus is on the working wall, the first set of tables can be as close as two or three feet from the wall.

✓ Pay attention to the suggestions of people working with you. Other people may see space options more quickly than you do.

EXAMPLE

I was invited to hold an all-day workshop in a school auditorium, complete with theater-style seats and no tables. None of the classrooms were big enough to hold all the people who were to attend the planning workshop. Finally we decided to use the cafeteria. The tables were for eating and had benches attached to them. However, one side wall in the cafeteria was completely blank. It worked perfectly. It was easy to arrange the tables so that everyone could sit around a table and see the working wall.

Things That Take Effort

PARTICIPATIVE PROCESSES

"The most effective meetings result in a meaningful, and ideally, tangible product ... A product that documents the decision or plan arrived at by the group reminds members of the group's consensus and serves as a guide for future action and progress evaluations." —Spencer

Materials

DESCRIPTION/BACKGROUND

Because you are after a tangible product, often tangible materials are needed for your meeting. Preparing the necessary materials beforehand further communicates how seriously you consider the time and participation of the people attending. Having everything at your fingertips creates a smooth meeting flow. Bringing the various materials and procuring enough of them enables the meeting to keep moving toward its focus.

People feel thought about and cared for when all of the materials are present for a meeting. It communicates that you feel the meeting is important. It is a piece to support the atmosphere that leads to consensus.

DID YOU KNOW?

- Simple, adequate materials result in less time wasted and increased team member confidence.
- Even adults enjoy using markers of varying colors.
- Creating a visible product during a team meeting gives people a great sense of accomplishment.

ACTIVITY
#**27**   *Materials*

This is another activity that requires your thought ahead of time and that enables your meeting to keep to its focus.

1. Ahead of time, look at the flow of your meeting.

2. List the materials you will need for each section of the meeting.

3. Place them close to where you stand or sit during the meeting.

4. Keep them in a place readily available for succeeding meetings.

Hints . . .

✓ **Some facilitators like to keep their materials together in a box which is always brought to the meeting.**

✓ **Looking at each piece of the meeting flow is crucial as different materials are often required for different sections of a meeting. In fact, one way to help the flow of a meeting is to use different methods or approaches for each section.**

✓ **A brainstorm may need chart paper, markers, and masking tape. A full workshop might need 5 x 8 cards, markers, and masking tape. Decision making might require chart paper, markers, and masking tape to work through the various options. Some activities are enhanced with different colors of markers available. Other activities need a special form on which people can write down their responses.**

EXAMPLE

Sample Materials List:

chart paper	easel with paper
masking tape	markers of assorted colors
5 x 8 cards	scratch paper—recycled paper
Post-it notes	folders
scissors	stapler and staples
ruler	correction fluid
pens and pencils	note paper

As you are planning your meeting, you can add materials to your time flow picture. For example, below is the time flow picture from Activity #25 (Time Flow Picture) with materials added.

TRAINING SESSION FLOW			
Intro.	Where we are on project timeline— THE BIG PICTURE		**2 min.**
	Quick Items	**Major Items**	**Minor Items**
A G E N D A	Review and Polishing Last Meeting's Major Product **12 min.**	Training Session on Next Phase of Finance Procedures **25 min.**	Content of Team Report to Department Meeting Minor Task Realignments **15 min.**
M A T E R I A L S	Typed Product—Copies for All	Chart Paper Markers Tape Sample Exercises	5 x 8 Cards Markers Tape Task Assignment Sheets
Concl.	Processing Question—What worked well for us in today's session?		**3 min.**

Things That Take Effort

PARTICIPATIVE PROCESSES

"It is up to the leader to carry out these processes competently and in a manner that is responsive to people's needs."
—Nelson, Burns, from Adams

Meeting Plan Forms

DESCRIPTION/BACKGROUND

For almost every meeting I plan, I use a simple meeting plan form to help me organize my thoughts and think about how I want the meeting to flow. This form is a guideline, not a rigid prescription. A meeting form is a tool for focusing your attention on the meeting at hand. Knowing you are going to fill out the meeting form helps you concentrate on the meeting. Also, some meetings may get unexpectedly complicated. Having that plan in front of you can help to keep you on track.

I also discovered that the written plan helps me to be more flexible. As long as I have made it through the main action or product, I can cut others short or postpone others until a future meeting. Without going through the prioritizing and planning, it might be much harder to be flexible in figuring out how to shorten something, cut it out, or postpone it.

DID YOU KNOW?

- It may take you more than one hour to carefully plan a one-hour meeting.
- Time spent after the meeting to think about what went well and how to improve your meetings is as valuable as the time you spend beforehand planning the meeting.
- Because a printed agenda is like a road map through your meeting, you want to make it easy to follow.

A C T I V I T Y

#28 *Meeting Plan Forms*

1. Note all the items you have decided to include in the meeting to be planned.

2. Using the meeting plan form, put them into the appropriate places.

3. The plan form has a place for the **Meeting Objective** and the **Experiential Goal**. The **Meeting Objective** is the primary goal or objective for the meeting—the most important thing you want to accomplish or the primary item you want people to know after the meeting. The **Experiential Goal** is what you want people to experience or decide by the end of the meeting. I find these to be critical guidelines in deciding what the meeting is about.

4. In addition to the simple contextual comments or team exercise at the beginning, I also conclude with one or more processing questions. The purpose of these is to help the team step back from the content of the meeting and think together about what has been going on—either the content or the methods being used. It is a great opportunity as openness increases to get some feedback on their sense of the meeting. Choose one or more of these:

   a. What has been important to you about this meeting?

   b. What do you like about what we have been doing?

   c. What don't you like? Why?

   d. What are your suggestions as to how we might proceed next?

   e. What methods seem to be working for us?

   f. What approaches do not seem to be working for us?

   g. What other methods or approaches do you think we should try?

Hints . . .

✓ As mentioned earlier, often I jot down the elements of the
meeting on small Post-it notes. Then I place the Post-it notes in
the appropriate slot on my meeting plan form so I can arrange
and rearrange them easily. When I am satisfied with the way it
looks, I fill out the form.

✓ Sometimes I use pencil on the form so that I can be free to
continue changing or adding things.

✓ I also find it helpful to make this plan at least a day ahead of time.
Very often when I wake up the day of the meeting, ideas suddenly
come that help me to polish and fine-tune my planning the day or
night before.

EXAMPLE

Note that this form is a little more detailed and complex than the
ones used in Activities #25 and #27.

<table>
<tr><th colspan="5">MEETING PLAN FORM</th></tr>
<tr><th>Intro.</th><th colspan="3">Meeting Objective</th><th>Experiential Goal</th></tr>
<tr><td>Remind people why this community input meeting is so important</td><td colspan="3">For the team to come up with a plan for a community input meeting on alternative time/ calendar options for school day/year</td><td>Heightened confidence on the team's part that they can pull off this meeting well</td></tr>
<tr><th rowspan="2">Content</th><th colspan="3">A G E N D A</th><th rowspan="2">Processing</th></tr>
<tr><th>Quick Items</th><th>Major Issues</th><th>Minor Issues</th></tr>
<tr><td>Quick conversation

What do we want to be the hallmarks of this meeting?</td><td>Who do we want to attend this meeting?

Where will it be held?

When shall we hold it?</td><td>What elements need to be part of this meeting?

Discern main points of agreement.

Lay out time flow.</td><td>Who will lead this meeting?

What tasks need to be done to get ready for this meeting?</td><td>Ask one or two of these questions:
What went well?

Where did we struggle?

Where did we come together and focus well as a group?</td></tr>
<tr><th>Materials</th><td>Chart paper
Tape
Markers</td><td>5 x 8 cards
Markers
Chart paper
Tape</td><td>Chart paper
Tape
Markers</td><td></td></tr>
<tr><th>Concl.</th><td colspan="4">Next meeting date/time</td></tr>
</table>

**PARTICIPATIVE
PROCESSES**

TAPPING THE GROUP AGREEMENT

INTRODUCTION TO AGREEMENT

Tapping the group agreement involves participative methods and processes to discern where the group agreement currently is. It also means constantly clarifying to the group what it currently has said yes to. The difficult aspect of this stage is that it goes way beyond merely taking a vote to see if the majority agree with something. Tapping the group agreement is about discerning which elements of a given topic the whole group is willing to run with and which ones the group is not ready to go with yet.

When I am facilitating, I work hard to avoid a situation calling for a vote. In the very beginning of the life of a group, it may be difficult to avoid. However, beyond such decisions as where to eat lunch, I avoid voting because it divides a group into two camps. Voting reveals the group's disagreements rather than enhancing or clarifying its agreements. Consequently, at every point, you can try to create options and solutions to which the whole group can affirm. Approaches that reveal the group agreement are at the very heart of the consensus-building process.

This is one of the most difficult arenas because it requires the most from the facilitator and relies so heavily on the intuitions of the facilitator. When can the group move on, or does the group need to spend more time on an issue? Because this often relies so much on

101

the judgment of the facilitator, it is the hardest to do while still guarding the participative processes. Thus it requires facilitator skill to reveal to the group its current thinking, options, and level of consensus.

"Postindustrial technology has also become so complex that it's impossible for managers to have all the answers."—Spencer

Workshop Flow

DESCRIPTION/BACKGROUND

This activity highlights the five basic steps to the flow of a participative workshop. When your intent is to gather the ideas from a group of people and help them see what their thinking and agreement is, these five basic sections are critical: Context, Idea Gathering, Organizing, Clarifying, and Processing.

This guideline provides you one possible framework to use when you are out to help a group see what it already knows and where its essential agreements already are. This is also a helpful guideline when you want to tap the wisdom of a group and then enable the group to see where its agreements are within its wide range of ideas.

DID YOU KNOW?

- Getting and utilizing participation is a highly structured process.
- Agreement does not come naturally to people raised on rugged individualism.
- A facilitator controls the process but not the content.

ACTIVITY

#*29* *Workshop Flow*

CONTEXT:

1. Set the stage. Remind people of the reason for this particular workshop.

2. State the one question (see Activity #18) or the particular focus of this workshop.

3. Remind people of the major steps of the process.

IDEA GATHERING:

1. Allow people time to think through their own responses individually.

2. Have people talk through their ideas in groups of three or four.

ORGANIZING:

1. Get the ideas out on chart paper or on 5 x 8 cards (see Activities #3 and #7).

2. As in Activity #3, if your list is on chart paper have the group intuitively discern the major arenas the data falls in.

3. If you are using cards, after getting the cards up front, do the clustering and the naming of temporary titles as described in Activity #7.

CLARIFYING:

1. Go over and polish the temporary titles by making sure the temporary title is still what the cluster is all about.

2. Then elicit two or three adjectives that really make the title crystal clear. *Funding* tells you the arena. *Diverse, Dependable Funding* tells you much more accurately what the group wants. Remember that this is the stage where real group agreement occurs. The discussions about these titles form the real consensus.

PROCESSING:

Choose one or two of these questions.

1. Content Processing

   a. Which arena speaks most to you in terms of your daily work?

   b. Which arena gets you most excited and intrigued?

   c. Which arena will have the most impact on the organization?

   d. What have we accomplished?

   e. What are some implications to the work we have done today?

2. Method Processing

   a. What methods or steps seemed to work for us today?

   b. Where did you get most involved?

   c. How could you use something like this in another situation?

Hints . . .

✓ **Be sure to allow people time to do individual thinking first.**

✓ **You can pursue some of the implications in greater detail by asking what next steps or decisions need to be made.**

✓ **As the leader, you are often tempted to comment on some of the data presented. Needless to say, the fewer comments you make the better. Value judgments about any of the responses are unnecessary as you seek the points of agreement revealed in the cluster titles.**

EXAMPLE

It often surprises me how certain people see this workshop flow happen a few times and immediately go out to do this right away in their work settings. After doing a series of workshops for the flight attendants division of an airline company, the two top division managers proceeded to hold input meetings throughout the country, using this workshop flow with thousands of flight attendants. They reported that the high quality of the input genuinely informed their continued planning and policy decisions. Idea Gathering, Organizing, and Clarifying worked for them.

For
The
Committed

**PARTICIPATIVE
PROCESSES**

"In companies that make things happen today, however, employees are seen as the company's most important resource in meeting the challenge of change."—Spencer

Three-to-One Scenarios

DESCRIPTION/BACKGROUND

When a group has gotten full clarity on an issue and is ready to move to mapping out some solutions, three smaller teams can create their own scenarios with what each team thinks are the critical pieces to the solution. Having each team present its own scenario will help the group discern the elements to winning solutions. This may also reveal, when actually written into the flow of a scenario form, which elements may not be appropriate or workable for the particular situation. Out of three possible scenarios, the group can then discern the one winning solution, perhaps with winning elements from all three suggested scenarios.

The key here is pulling the aspects to a possible solution together into a scenario. In other words, it is almost as if each team is charged to write the script or the plot of one possible way to solve the issue including as many of the values as previously discerned.

DID YOU KNOW?

- The journey to consensus begins with small steps of agreement.
- Helping people see the variety of options actually helps them see the direction they really want to go.
- Seeing a variety of options helps clarify the values you have for a desired solution.

ACTIVITY

#30 *Three-to-One Scenarios*

1. Divide the group into three teams.

2. Charge each team to come up with a possible scenario that would satisfy the constraints of the situation.

3. Have each team record the script for its scenario on a piece of chart paper.

4. Have each team then present its scenario. Recognize each team with a round of applause.

5. Process all of the presentations together with one or two of these questions:

   a. Which aspects of these scenarios stand out for you?

   b. Which one(s) interest you the most?

   c. Where do you see some connections or common elements in the scenario presentations?

   d. Where are the major differences?

   e. What are the implications of each of these scenarios?

   f. How would you characterize each one, or title each one?

   g. As you look through all of these together, what seem to be elements of the one winning solution?

6. Put the winning elements on 5 x 8 cards or on a piece of chart paper.

7. Keep working with the elements until the pieces and the flow of the winning solution come into focus.

8. Suggest that this one winning solution stand for a few minutes or a few days so that the team can come back to it, examine it, and polish it.

9. Process how the group currently feels about the winning solution. Check and see if there are any major gaps or holes in the winning solution.

10. Conclude the activity with one or two final processing questions:

    a. What steps in this process seemed to work especially well for us?

    b. What aspects of this product are you particularly pleased with?

    c. What happened to us as a group while we worked on this?

    d. In what kind of situation could you use this process again?

Hints . . .

✓ It is very helpful to have some outside data or additional information about other people's possible solutions.

✓ As they begin, many groups may feel tremendous ambiguity about creating a scenario. Allow the group to experience that ambiguity fully so that they may have the possibility of experiencing a breakthrough.

✓ If possible, allow time between initially creating the winning solution and having a finished product. Even overnight allows the group to get some distance. That allows additional opportunity to enhance the solution, deal with some inconsistencies in the solution, and create buy-in where there is not yet a total buy-in. Very often people react negatively because they have not had a chance to absorb the full impact of the solution and think it through for themselves.

EXAMPLE

A group I worked with was trying to find a solution to an emotionally charged issue. They already had input from five community focus groups, one teacher focus group, several classes, and a local school council meeting.

The whole group took the data and first discerned all the possible solution pieces or elements. Then using these as "ingredients for a recipe," so to speak, each team chose various pieces or elements and created a solution scenario.

After each team presented its scenario, the group fashioned a winning solution with elements from each of the presented scenarios. This became the structure of their proposed solution.

"As they begin to feel that they and their ideas really make a difference to the company, passive workers become actively engaged in the creative change process."—Spencer

Cooperative Writing Workshop

DESCRIPTION/BACKGROUND

This activity enables a group of people to write a full document in teams in a way that the final product has flow and continuity. The final product often addresses the team with its comprehensiveness and sense of unity. Many people discover their group is more connected than they thought after experiencing the successful completion of this cooperative writing activity.

The key to this activity is dividing both the document and the group into workable parts. For example, fifteen people could make five teams of three, which also suggests dividing the document into five pieces.

DID YOU KNOW?

- Writing about the group's points of consensus helps a group to connect the points of agreement and deepen the foundation of its consensus.

- Once a group has a common experience creating points of consensus, its writing is amazingly consistent.

- Writing about the group's points of consensus is a structured format that enables the group to get penetrating clarity on its thinking.

ACTIVITY

#31 *Cooperative Writing Workshop*

1. After the group has experienced something like a workshop or input of data together, you may want the group to do some writing together.

2. If the group has not already created the structure of the document to be written through a workshop, hold a workshop to create the actual structure of the document itself. Very often after I lead a workshop on the vision (Activity #17), the group wants to write a mission statement built on the elements discerned in that workshop.

3. Suggest to the group a common structure to each piece of the document, e.g., an introduction, a definition of this piece, some examples of what this piece is about, some implications of this, and finally in the conclusion, a word about its significance or importance.

4. You might even prepare ahead of time a form that each team could use in the writing of its section.

5. Divide the group into the same number of teams as the pieces of the document.

6. Suggest a reasonable time limit—from twenty minutes for a paragraph to several days for a chapter-length writing.

7. If the document is short enough, have the teams read aloud the document in its entirety. If the document is too long, have each team read samples of its writing. Find an appropriate way to recognize each team's contribution.

8. After the reading, allow the group to step back and process what it has heard with one or two of these questions:

   a. What did you notice about the document we created?

   b. What words or phrases did you appreciate?

   c. What intrigued or surprised you?

   d. As a whole, what are some of the major ideas this document communicates?

   e. What are our next steps now with this document?

Hints . . .

✓ I would only do this if the group has some common experience on which to base their writing—for example, having gone through a workshop together. Otherwise you risk the chance of the writing sounding as if it comes from conflicting and contradictory perspectives.

✓ When the group begins with a common experience of a workshop or some kind of common input, the group is able to write with smooth flow and continuity.

EXAMPLE

A commission on a small city council had amassed a huge three hundred-page document representing its plans for some major rehabilitation in the downtown area. They were concerned that people had lost the sense of what the whole planning was about. First I led a workshop like the vision workshop trying to capture the hallmarks of the vision outlined in the document. Then, the group wrote a summary paragraph on each of the eight major elements of their vision. The initial workshop and the writing took less than two hours to accomplish.

When the members heard the summary document they had written, they were astounded. Many commented that it was only then that they understood all the work they had been doing.

For
The
Committed

PARTICIPATIVE
PROCESSES

"Workers who contribute their input to a plan feel pride of ownership. They become committed to the plan's success and see themselves as integral to its execution."—Spencer

Mapping the Road to Agreement

DESCRIPTION/BACKGROUND

There are times when the group is just not ready to come to agreement. When you have the option of a little more time and can schedule a follow-up meeting, you can conclude the workshop by asking, "What do we need to settle in order to come to an agreement?" or "What are the items we need more clarity on before this group can reach an agreement?" Following that, teams can be created to handle each major item with the understanding that they will come to the next meeting with information or with a model which will lead the group to agreement.

The facilitator is using the group's thinking to create its own pathway to agreement. When a group gets into a morass, the pathway to agreement is clouded and unclear. The facilitator is literally helping the group lay its own tracks to come to agreement.

DID YOU KNOW?

- The solution to conflict lies within the group itself.
- The people closest to the conflict within the group are the very people who know the way to agreement.
- Seeing the stages on the road to agreement makes consensus feel more possible.

ACTIVITY

#32 *Mapping the Road to Agreement*

Knowing *when* to use this activity is tricky. This is not to be used to help the group escape from the demands of coming to agreement. But, if there is time, it is helpful to use this when a group appears to be at an immense impasse. The strategy is an attempt to help the group grasp what is really standing in the way of some genuine agreement.

1. Begin by helping the group state where the current points of agreement are.

2. Help the group name where the current unsettled points are.

3. Do cardstorming or a brainstormed list of what needs to be settled before the group can reach agreement (Activities #3 and #7). You may have only a few items. If you have several items you will want to use the list or the cards to discern the major clusters of three to five larger issues.

4. Have the group choose the subteams that will deal with those issues and come prepared with information or a model for agreement by the next meeting.

5. At the next meeting, have each group report.

6. By this time the group will have all the necessary information or clarity needed to proceed and complete the agreements needed. Perhaps the Three-to-One Scenario activity could be employed at this point (Activity #30).

Hints . . .

✓ The importance of small teams here is for pulling together some consensus within the small teams before coming back to the larger group. When a group reaches a morass, for some reason individuals become reluctant to compromise and come to consensus. Therefore, this strategy allows them to return to a small group and reach a consensus there first.

✓ Particularly with a group that has been functioning for some time already, the facilitator needs to step back at every point of a morass and discern what is really blocking the consensus. Consensus building relies so much on trust. It is always helpful to ask whether the major issue blocking the consensus is a content one or a group dynamic one. This strategy provides an opportunity for the next stage of trust to occur.

EXAMPLE

One social service agency began a meeting I facilitated with an assumption by a few that they were going to carry out a very controversial project which would definitely elicit hostile responses from the local neighborhood. As the meeting progressed, it became clear that the group itself had not come to any agreement that this was the way to proceed. In fact as we spoke together an alternative strategy began to emerge. Yet the original few were not ready to give up their controversial strategy.

In order to come to agreement, they needed to know what various constituencies would think about their new alternative strategies. One team was sent to find out which of the two strategies would get the most support from the local city council. Another was sent to find out which strategy would make the most sense to the clients they wanted to serve. A third group was to check with the members not present at the meeting. When they convened two weeks later, the overwhelming support for the new alternative (and less controversial) strategy allowed everyone to come to agreement on which way to proceed.

FOR
THE
COMMITTED

**PARTICIPATIVE
PROCESSES**

"Effective participation results in a greater flow of ideas and positions and requires a sound means to deal with the differences that emerge."—Blake, Mouton, and Allen

Agreement: State and Restate

DESCRIPTION/BACKGROUND

From time to time I state the points of agreement so far. I remind team members of the things we have agreed to say no to and the things we have agreed to say yes to. Furthermore, I clarify what we have not yet agreed upon. It is helpful to remind a group that is overwhelmed with what is still unresolved of what progress has already been made. Because the group is always progressing in its deliberations, a statement of where it is always reveals the progress it is making.

DID YOU KNOW?

- Reminding people where they already have created agreement encourages them to make the next step of agreement.
- Stating and restating exactly where a group is keeps it focused on the next step of agreement.
- Stating and restating points of agreement communicate to the group that you as the leader are paying close attention to everything that is going on.

ACTIVITY

#33   *Agreement: State and Restate*

During the meeting in which you are seeking agreement, every few minutes state to the group exactly where they are in the whole flow of coming to agreement.

1. For example, on the simpler side, if you are planning an agenda for a meeting, you can repeat the pieces that already have agreement and point out what is still unclear: "So far we agree on the introduction, the presentation of data, and a time for questions. What we are not clear on yet is precisely about which issue we want to get input. What is your thinking now on that?"

2. On the more difficult side, if you are trimming $500,000 from your budget, I would make two kinds of comments:

   "So far we have decided to save $100,000 by eliminating new purchases and $50,000 through a percentage cut of everyone's budget."

   or

   "So far we have decided not to touch benefits, supplies, or salaries."

   And, "Remember as we proceed, these are the six values and guidelines we have established for this whole budget-trimming process."

   I would even go a step further and have chart paper up front to document first the decisions which have already been made, e.g., the $100,000 and the $50,000 and the values and guidelines originally established to help the group through the process.

   "So what are some possible sources for the remaining $350,000?"

Hints . . .

✓ **You may find it helpful to use both visual and auditory reinforcements here.**

✓ **The more complex the decisions, the more a group needs cues to remind it of where it has come from and where it is heading.**

✓ **You may need to implement some elements of Activity #32 (Mapping the Road to Agreement) before a final resolution can occur.**

EXAMPLE

I was invited to lead a workshop with a group that reportedly had two very divergent views about how to proceed. My first step was to clarify for them the one question both sides were trying to answer. Then, working with the group, I helped them to lay out visually the two clashing directions. By constantly stating and restating both where there was agreement and where there was not agreement, I at least got agreement on the common question, the two divergent solutions, and their implications. This meeting clarified that one solution saved money in the short run but the second solution would eventually have to be pursued anyway. I decided to use a second meeting to proceed further. In a few days, without the second meeting, I was surprised to hear that the second solution had been chosen with full agreement.

INDIVIDUAL COMMITMENT

"To achieve the level of involvement . . . which is necessary to become appropriately flexible, quality-conscious, and thence competitive, we must organize as much as possible around teams, to achieve enhanced focus, task orientation, innovativeness, and individual commitment."
(Peters, 1987, p. 296)

I deas alone cannot fully link people together. What connects people is not mere ideas but deep personal commitments. Commitments involve feeling, passion, and drive. Ideas only bring heads together. The head is not the source of feeling, passion, and drive. When you feel someone else's commitment toward something you also have committed to, you become connected to the other person with more than your head.

So how does real consensus happen? It begins at the commitment level. That person whose political party is different from mine is deeply committed to a safe environment in our community. I want that too. This other person whose management style is opposite from mine desperately wants employee morale to increase. So do I. Connections grow. The potential for consensus rises when you discover that someone is deeply committed to that which you are committed. You may even step back and examine that person's ideas with a new perspective. This examination of others' perspectives is critical for consensus because what genuinely drives and concerns people is often much more similar and concrete than mere ideological differences. When these deep commitments begin to speak to each other in a dialogue, mutual respect grows and energy for the task deepens.

This shared commitment is what Adams suggests can grow to a point of being able to shield and protect the individuals in the midst of the stress and burdens of carrying out the group's tasks. It is as if the more you are reminded of the commitment of the group, the more you are able to squeeze out more ounces of energy, the more you are able to withstand the criticism and cynicism you may be meeting from outside of the group. Individual commitment provides the stamina that keeps a group moving toward consensus.

Individual commitment has to do with creating the atmosphere that treats every individual as a valued human being. The challenge is fostering an atmosphere people are frankly delighted to be a part of. When this kind of honoring of the individual happens, energy for the task and energy toward consensus are practically boundless.

The atmosphere of commitment gives people the courage to risk consensus. An atmosphere of commitment is created as many individual commitments merge together into a whole environment. This environment that supports each person's deep commitments calls forth individual support for the whole group task. In so doing it enhances the courage to risk on behalf of the whole. It calls forth a daring that may not have been present before, a daring to move beyond what anyone individually may have been willing to venture previously. When an atmosphere of commitment is experienced, people begin to feel a sense of safety. When this happens, walls begin to crumble and barriers come down.

Earlier we stated the connection between involvement and commitment. We are now adding a third dimension: Involvement, Commitment, and Risk. When courage and risk are called for, first work on involvement and commitment. Risk and courage will naturally follow, and consensus will emerge almost without effort. Consensus can begin with some very small decisions. Celebrate those. And gradually, the scope and depth of consensus will increase to the critical and most controversial areas.

INDIVIDUAL COMMITMENT

ELICITING DETAILED ASSIGNMENTS

INTRODUCTION TO ASSIGNMENTS

Clear-cut assignments make commitment concrete. Without clear assignments, there is no way to gauge individual commitment. Vague assignments pave the way to vague commitment, to say nothing of immense frustration because nothing seems to get done.

Because consensus is founded on concrete commitment, detailed and specific assignments are part of what indicates your group's potential for consensus. As people witness the completion of tasks, trust builds and again the potential for genuine consensus increases.

A supportive atmosphere surrounding concrete assignments is crucial. People fear that they will be held personally accountable for the results of their particular assignments. This is where the next section on the collaborative teams comes in. Although an individual name is put down next to each assignment, the team is ultimately responsible for its accomplishment. A successful team holds the tension between individual accountability and team support.

121

"Individuals committed to a vision beyond their self-interest find they have energy not available when pursuing narrower goals, as will organizations that tap this level of commitment." —Senge

Task Volunteers

DESCRIPTION/BACKGROUND

Opening up the floor for volunteers to complete various tasks communicates to the group full confidence that it can figure out how to accomplish these tasks. In other words, there are times when volunteers are more likely to get the job done than people who may be assigned against their will.

I am sure there are times when this may not be practical. Furthermore, there often are tasks uniquely suited to certain people. Again, the team or work colleagues often know that and suggest that the people most qualified to do a task do it.

As a rule, I suggest that if people have been participating all along in defining and laying out the steps of the projects, then they will also see which steps will realistically fit into their schedules and other time demands. My experience is that when people have a chance to participate in the full context and to get their ideas into the formation of the necessary projects, they are always willing to put themselves behind the successful completion of the projects. Volunteering for the tasks eliminates one source of excuses.

DID YOU KNOW?

- When people are involved in planning from the start, many actually want to help complete the project.
- You tend to pour extra energy into tasks you want to do.
- Task volunteering creates a snowball effect—each new step volunteered for creates a milieu that calls for more volunteering.

ACTIVITY

#34 *Task Volunteers*

This activity rests on the assumption that your team wants to see the project completed. Your style here communicates absolute trust in their competence and desire to finish the project.

1. From the start, the leader needs to communicate that this team is an action team. The team members have a right to know that they have been considered from the start to be part of the implementation.

2. The team needs to be a part of both creating the big chunks of the task and of the breakdown of the task into implementing steps.

3. At this point, an appropriate question is, "How shall we divide up the task to get all the steps accomplished?"

4. It may happen that one or two difficult steps are left without volunteers. In this case perhaps two people will take responsibility for completing a task that one person was not willing to volunteer for. Or perhaps you need to ask if the responsibility can be divided into even smaller chunks.

5. Once these steps are passed out, as a general rule, the leader's only concern is the *completion* of that task—not the *method* for completing the task. This demonstrates the leader's trust in the group.

6. It is crucial to set the next meeting time and to clarify exactly what is expected to be accomplished by that meeting.

Hints . . .

✓ From the start, people need to know they are part of the implementation. It is not helpful to invite people to a planning meeting that they think is only to gather their ideas for a plan when you are really counting on them to carry out the plan.

✓ If there is reluctance to volunteer, let the rest of the members push each other on this as much as possible. Team members will be more receptive to their peers pushing them rather than a traditional top-down assignment.

✓ At the end the leader might ask, "Does all this seem realistic?" If there are concerns, let the group handle them.

✓ Ideally, the leader has enough rapport with the group that spot checking between meetings will be seen as a method of support. If there are implementation problems, the question from the leader is, "How can the team help you?" or "How can I help you?" rather than "Why haven't you been able to get this done?"

EXAMPLE

I worked with a group that entered a planning workshop very disgruntled over its work situation. There had been a variety of issues and complaints that we worked very hard to get out on the table during the planning. After an excellent planning workshop, it came time to divide into teams. Would one person make the assignments? Would we take volunteers (as I am prone to suggest)?

I was amazed at the group's own suggestion. They wanted to put everyone's name in a hat and draw names one at a time and alternately fill each team. Those randomly selected teams have been highly functional ever since. The group decided that this option would demonstrate its own commitment to start in a radically new way, thereby breaking with any tendency to operate in cliques or by friendships. This symbolized an incredible depth of individual commitment and trust.

"As we make and keep commit-ments . . . we begin to establish an inner integrity that gives us the awareness of self-control and the courage and strength to accept more of the responsibility for our own lives." —Covey

What/Who/When Cards

DESCRIPTION/BACKGROUND

Cards can be used to record the individual steps needed to carry out an assignment. The step, the name of the person who is going to do it, and the completion date can all be written on one card.

These same cards can be used in conjunction with Activity #36, Timelines. They can be put onto the timeline and then moved around as adjustments are necessary.

The use of these cards is another way to keep the tasks before each individual and to keep before everyone's eyes the commitments individuals are making toward accomplishing a task.

DID YOU KNOW?

• Many people need help imagining all the little steps involved to complete a project.

• What may seem like time-consuming specificity on the front end saves a great deal of time down the line.

• What/Who/When cards leave little room for wondering how something is going to get done.

ACTIVITY

#35

What/Who/When Cards

1. Prepare the blank What/Who/When cards ahead of time.

2. Pass out the cards to each group.

3. For each project, have everyone brainstorm the ten to fifteen steps it will take to accomplish the project.

4. Write the steps on the cards, one step per card.

5. Have the teams fill out the "who" and "when" categories. Have individuals volunteer for the tasks to be done and then write their names and the completion dates on the cards.

6. Having the teams lay their cards out on the table or on the wall may help to clarify the flow or provide additional insights as to effective implementation.

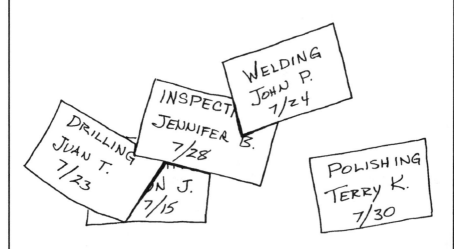

Hints . . .

✓ Very often I have groups that initially write only one or two cards to carry out a project. Then I ask questions such as the following: "When will you decide where the meeting is going to be?" "How are you going to let people know about the meeting?" "Where is the meeting going to be?" "Are there going to be refreshments?" "Who is going to clean up?" Suddenly it dawns on people the myriad of steps it takes to implement any project successfully.

✓ Completing these cards helps the group see what lies ahead. Again, ask the question of realism frequently. If one person has too much to accomplish, figure that out ahead of time if possible and shift some assignments around to make the responsibilities more realistic.

EXAMPLE

This is one step of many in planning a commemorative dinner.

WHAT	
Contact main speaker	
WHO	**WHEN**
Jack	By March 3

#36

Simple
Things
To
Do

INDIVIDUAL
COMMITMENT

*"The Implementation Timeline ...
will serve as the checkpoint for
future review sessions."*
—Spencer

Timelines

DESCRIPTION/BACKGROUND

A visual timeline can be an extremely valuable tool in laying out the
tasks ahead. I suggest doing a timeline for several months or a year
to give people an accurate understanding of the larger picture. After
that, moving to a smaller time period will allow the kind of detail
people need to make realistic judgments about the feasibility and
realism of what they want to accomplish.

It is easy for people to make promises in a vacuum: "Of course I
can do these three steps." Those three steps may be relatively simple.
But what about the fifty other tasks that have not been included on
the timeline? A comprehensive and complete timeline, not just for
one team but for all the teams in a group, will help everyone see the
big picture and may even avoid conflicts.

DID YOU KNOW?

- Graphic timelines can reveal time conflicts early enough to change your plans.
- Time openings revealed on a graphic timeline allow you to use that time instead of cramming things into the same time block.
- Graphic timelines are a guideline or a support not a rule book cracking a whip over you.

ACTIVITY

#**36** *Timelines*

1. Using 5 x 8 cards, lay out the major projects or tasks down the left side of a wall and the months or weeks across the top.

2. Have the team write out the steps for each task and place them under the appropriate week or month column. See Activity #35, What/Who/When Cards.

3. When the entire picture is up on the wall, ask the team, "What do you notice?" or "What is this timeline revealing to us?"

4. Again, this can be extremely informative. If the bulk of the team's steps or accomplishments occurs in the same week, that can be seen here and altered. It may also reveal that every team has chosen the same week for a major emphasis or effort. This may need to be changed.

5. Ask, "What changes would make this timeline more realistic?"

6. You might also ask, "Now that you see the whole picture, what duplicate steps do you see across the teams?" or "What steps could be combined?"

7. It is very tempting to make helpful suggestions yourself. But asking the question puts the responsibility back on the team to decide.

Hints . . .

✓ Noting not just the flow of each project but the flow of each project in relationship to every other project is crucial here. That is why the visual picture can be so enabling.

✓ Once the entire timeline has been reviewed and polished, I ask the group to step back and imagine it is the end of the timeline and most everything has been accomplished. Then I ask, "What new position will we be in if all this gets done?" This helps to put people in a stance of victory which can sustain them over the accomplishment of these projects.

EXAMPLE

TIMELINE					
	AUG.	**SEPT.**	**OCT.**	**NOV.**	**DEC.**
PROJECT ONE	☐☐☐ ☐☐	☐ ☐ ☐	☐	☐	
PROJECT TWO	☐ ☐	☐ ☐	☐☐☐ ☐ ☐	☐ ☐	☐
PROJECT THREE	☐ ☐	☐ ☐ ☐	☐	☐ ☐ ☐ ☐	☐
PROJECT FOUR	☐	☐	☐ ☐ ☐	☐ ☐	☐☐☐ ☐ ☐

Simple
Things
To
Do

**INDIVIDUAL
COMMITMENT**

*"Work flows from and is a
natural outgrowth of a desire for
challenge, stimulation, feedback,
success, and association with
others in meaningful activity."*
—Ritscher from Adams

Attendance

DESCRIPTION/BACKGROUND

This activity suggests the importance of acknowledging who is
around the table and who is not. I am not suggesting that every
person's name be read, but rather that particular mention can be
made of all who are not present and why they are not present.

    This is a simple way to dramatize that every single individual on
the team is important to the task (and to consensus). We may be
tempted to gloss over people's absences, but to do so communicates
that those people are not important—or that ultimately individuals
are not important to the whole team. Everyone on the team deserves
to know where the absent people are. This honors those who have
been able to carry out their commitment to be present.

DID YOU KNOW?

- Each human being who makes it to your meeting is crucial for the success of
  the whole task.

- People are willing to work hard in a meeting when they are clear why others
  are not able to make the meeting.

- People need reminders that even though one or two may be absent, it is still
  possible to get the necessary work accomplished.

#*37* *Attendance*

In one way this activity is simple. Yet the absence of people can subtly drain the group. Unless we say otherwise, absence can communicate that the absent person is not committed to the team.

1. For example, say: "As you know, John is out sick today, and Sally is at the district office in a meeting with the manager. Both of them said they would call me tomorrow and get filled in on our meeting today."

2. Continue by saying: "We are not all here, but I believe the rest of us can carry out what we need to do today" or "It is hard when we are not all here but let's see how as one team we can get our tasks done today."

Hints . . .

✓ How we handle absences sets the tone of a meeting. By taking absences too lightly, we subtly devalue a team member: "John never says much when he is here anyway" or "It is O.K., we do not really need Sally today."

✓ Another temptation is to use an absence as an excuse for venting frustration or anger: "How can we get our work done if all these people do not show up?" or "What is the matter, don't John and Sally realize how much work we have to finish?" Such statements communicate a lot about our views of John and Sally.

✓ Many people feel that any effort in this direction treats the team and its members as little children. Acknowledging who is there and who is not somehow demeans people. To the contrary, I suggest this as a powerful tool, when done well, in honoring the individuals who are expending their commitment and energy for the tasks at hand.

EXAMPLE

Many times when I teach a course with thirty or forty people in it, a person will come up and explain that he or she has to leave early for a particular commitment. I make sure each person who takes the time to talk to me knows how much I appreciate this. I explain what is being covered so they will know what to ask their team members about when they return. Frequently, I ask for an additional assignment. I never say, "Oh, well, there are so many people here, I would not have noticed anyway" or "Didn't you know when you signed up for this course that you had to be here the full time?"

It is time to communicate to people that we know they are intelligent, important people who live in a swirl of overwhelming responsibilities. The situation can be very different, however, if you know beforehand that you are dealing with someone who is shirking responsibility. In this case, I would offer this person two alternatives, both of which are acceptable, each of which would demonstrate picking up more responsibility.

#38

"Transformational leaders do not fall into the trap of treating people as cogs in the mechanism. They treat people as individuals who are seeking their own satisfaction and fulfillment."
—Ritscher from Adams

Assignment Chart

DESCRIPTION/BACKGROUND

This activity suggests that assignments be written out or typed up and made available in a chart for all to have. The names of each person on the team need to be printed out on a list. The particular tasks, steps, and the names of those who will be doing them are written out or typed up to be passed out or posted in a place visible to everyone.

A printed chart informs everyone of what fellow team members are doing. This is a way of supporting everyone's commitment. People often put forth a little extra effort when they know that everyone else knows they have agreed and are responsible for a task or project. In addition, people often put forth extra effort because of how much effort everyone else is also putting forth.

DID YOU KNOW?

• People are empowered when they have a clear idea what everyone else is working on.

• People are reminded of the whole task when they see the full picture represented in a comprehensive assignment chart.

• The assignment chart objectively communicates to each person that everyone is depending on each particular task in order for the whole project to get done.

ACTIVITY

#38 *Assignment Chart*

1. As teams are laying out their implementation steps or as they are filling out their What /Who/ When cards (Activity #35), have them fill in an assignment chart.

2. After the teams have reported and adjustments have been made, collect these charts and have them typed up.

3. Make sure that everyone gets a copy of these charts.

PROJECT	New Marketing Brochure	
STEPS	**WHO**	**WHEN**
1. Finalize product name	John	April 3
2. Write descriptive paragraphs	Beth	April 10
3. Get info to lay-out person	Dan	April 12
4. Get first draft back from lay-out person	Dan	April 15
5. Revise the final draft	Beth	April 17
6. Draft back to lay-out person	Dan	April 19
7. Pick up revised brochure	Dan	April 23
8. Get approval from manager	John	April 24
9. Send to printer	Vicki	April 25
10. Pick up brochures from printer	Vicki	May 1
11. Send to mail house for mailing	Vicki	May 2
12. Check to see if brochure has been received	Dan	May 10

Hints . . .

✓ An assignment chart is a tool to enhance individual commitment as well as to help the group remember who is to do what.

✓ Making sure that everyone has a copy is a great way to dramatize the commitments many have made to getting things done. It is even more impressive if the assignments have been made by the team and not by one person in a top-down way. This clearly shows the involvement of every individual on the team.

✓ Individual commitments can be enhanced when this tool is used to strengthen and support the team. Avoid using this as a tool to beat people over the head with a task or project not yet completed as this will create an unwillingness on the part of people to link their names with specific tasks.

EXAMPLE

Before working for a company, I was given a three-ring binder with every team's plans. A copy of this binder went to everyone. When it came time to report, each person had a binder and could follow through on how much of the plan had been accomplished.

The plans were very specific. Many included graphs and charts that clarified the progress they intended to make throughout the implementation of their plans. These could be compared to the graphs and charts passed out at the conclusion of this planning period.

Crucial to this coming off in the celebrative way it did was the nonjudgmental attitude that permeated the room. If things had not gone according to plan, people were asked the reason and how their future plans could benefit from the work of the previous time period. This atmosphere went a long way to deepening individual commitment.

INDIVIDUAL COMMITMENT

EXPANDING PERSONAL RECOGNITION

INTRODUCTION TO RECOGNITION

Recognition is a *lateral* form of honoring the people working on your team. In the past, honoring always went to people hierarchically higher than you, to people older than you, or it went down in the form of reward and recognition. In this age of all people coming to a new sense of their own self-worth, motivation to work together increases as people sense their contributions are understood and valued by those with whom they are working side by side.

In other words, an environment that recognizes and appreciates each person's individual gifts fosters and nurtures individual commitment. We expect more and more responsibility of individuals today. People can actually increase their commitment as personal recognition is expanded.

Consensus is difficult if not impossible to achieve in an atmosphere of distrust and an environment that denigrates individuals. In such an atmosphere, personal survival quickly becomes the key goal. Rapidly a milieu grows in which the norm is to do only the very minimum of what is required. Deep consensus will more likely emerge if people experience recognition of their gifts, for in such an atmosphere people will increasingly want the team with its plans and projects to win.

Things
That
Take
Effort

**INDIVIDUAL
COMMITMENT**

*"Unprecedented information-
sharing, interaction, and
recognition are required to
induce the attitude change and
horizontal communication
necessary to foster widespread
involvement and commitment."*
—Peters

Specific Praise

DESCRIPTION/BACKGROUND

Praise is often difficult to offer. There is a mindset that says: "Why praise people for just doing their jobs?" or "Work is its own reward, so praise does not need to be offered" or "If I praise, then people will relax and not work." All of these create an atmosphere that is stingy on praise.

Other people find it easy to praise. They are always saying: "That's a great job" or "You are the best secretary I have ever had." This kind of praise may make both the giver and the receiver feel good for a moment but this kind of praise is not very helpful.

Specific praise pinpoints the precise action or accomplishment that merits praise and names it to the individual. This fosters a genuineness and believability in the interaction. Specific praise helps people know exactly the kind of action, activity, or accomplishment to perform again. People have a right to learn where they stand more than once a year during a performance appraisal.

DID YOU KNOW?

- A minute of praise and recognition can result in an hour of extra energy toward the task.

- Even if praise and recognition sound phony at first, gradually they become more genuine.

- Praise and appreciation are contagious—they can spread not only through the company but even to the clients.

ACTIVITY
#39 *Specific Praise*

Because this type of recognition is not natural for most of us right away, you may need to practice this ahead of time.

1. There are several models, but one I find helpful is from Robert Bolton's book (*People Skills*, 1979, p. 183):

    When you . . . I feel . . . because . . .

2. When you first try this, you may want to write it out ahead of time to clarify to yourself what you want to say.

3. It might look like the following:

    a. "When you finished that report two days early, I was delighted, because that allowed the department heads to read and approve it before I had to send it on to the Regional Manager."

    b. "When you led the meeting so smoothly, I was delighted, because people left feeling they knew the important information and were ready to make a decision on the matter next week ."

    c. "When you took the extra time to meet with that upset client, I was pleased, because that demonstrated that we care about customer service."

Hints . . .

✓ Some people are so unaccustomed to hearing such direct communication that it might be necessary to repeat the praise once or
twice until you get a clue that your point has been clearly heard
and understood.

✓ Needless to say, this same pattern can be used to communicate
something which needs to be corrected to an employee or fellow
worker.

✓ Some workplaces establish an "employee-of-the-month" program, complete with a luncheon with the boss and perhaps other
recognition tokens. If such a program is used, make sure that the
specifics of the employee's performance are highlighted so that
everyone understands the kinds of concrete actions that are being
celebrated and rewarded in your particular job environment.

EXAMPLE

The following represents how one group figured out how to give
specific praise. Your team will need to experiment with what is
appropriate and works for it. Every three months, The IRI Group
(International Renewal Institute) passes out three kinds of awards to
its employees: Special Contribution—for contributions beyond the
call of duty; Team Building—for efforts that enable a team or teams;
and Peak Performance—for contributions that illustrate individual
effort for the good of the company. Each award specifically men-
tions the particular activity or accomplishment that merited the
award. At the end of the year, the number and kind of awards
received determine the number of tickets that each employee earns
toward a drawing for the yearly company employee prize. Just
receiving the awards throughout the year increases good feelings
about work. The prize at the end of the year is something concrete
that symbolizes the company's commitment to the employees. As
you walk through the office, you see that many employees have
posted their awards by their desks.

140

". . . celebrations have a powerful contribution to make."
—Owen

Individual Celebrations

DESCRIPTION/BACKGROUND

Individual celebrations—either those related to personal life or to work and professional life—are critical to acknowledge. Many teams are already good at noting people's birthdays, a degree received, or a promotion earned. In addition, a specific victory with a challenging project, a leading role in pulling off a major event, and an article written for a magazine can also be causes for celebration.

In our work-permeated life, I once heard someone say that you just cannot have too many celebrations. When something out of the ordinary happens, even five minutes of celebration can lift everyone's spirits for the next twenty-four hours.

DID YOU KNOW?

- An appropriate celebration for an individual's accomplishment or birthday is an opportunity to show appreciation for that person's unique gifts.

- Individual celebrations are opportunities for everyone to step back and think about their own life journey.

- Small, appropriate celebrations that feed people's connections to each other not only add building blocks for consensus but add motivation for accomplishing the tasks as well.

ACTIVITY

#40 *Individual Celebrations*

1. Customarily, we think of food and drink when it comes time for celebration. These things do wonders.

2. In addition, a key question or two in the midst of noting someone's individual celebration can cause everyone to stand back and reflect a moment:

    a. What does it mean to you now that you have your master's degree?

    b. What has been the most significant event for you in this last year?

    c. What are you looking forward to in the year to come?

    d. What do you feel has been one of your key accomplishments in your role as department head?

    e. What did you discover as you wrote that article?

    f. What did you learn about teams as your team successfully completed that difficult task?

    g. What kept you going?

3. Five or ten minutes at the beginning or end of a meeting can be used from time to time for celebrating. For some it seems like time wasted. For the wise facilitator, it is the stuff that keeps individuals motivated and energized.

Hints . . .

✓ Key questions that cause people to think back and reflect can begin to call forth responses of what is giving meaning and worth to people in the midst of often-hectic lives. People are eager to hear their colleagues speak about these things.

✓ Although something like this at every team meeting may seem impractical, something like this every month is not too often.

✓ This calls for you as the facilitator to be alert to the informal conversations going on as people gather or during break times so that opportunities for authentic individual celebrations can be capitalized on when they occur.

EXAMPLE

A team member with whom I worked immigrated to the United States from another country and received his doctorate after a great deal of study in this country. We decided to hold a small celebration. At that time, we posed to him the question of the meaning of this degree for him. While acknowledging that the work had been hard, especially working in English as his second language, he further commented, "Because of the upheaval in my country, I can never return there. I have no other place to go. I am grateful for this place to work." That is the kind of reflective comment that can push the thinking of everyone listening. I know I started to wonder if I could endure experiences like that team member had and still be as gracious and affirming of life as he was. Would I have had the stamina to work as hard as he had? This kind of comment further calls forth deep appreciation for the spirit of such a human being. As I said earlier, it may take only five or ten minutes, but a lot can happen to people when such opportunities occur.

Things
That
Take
Effort

INDIVIDUAL COMMITMENT

"There is nothing more important to an individual committed to his or her own growth than a supportive environment." —Senge

Training, Coaching, or Project Feedback

DESCRIPTION/BACKGROUND

Occasionally there are times you are called on to give feedback to a training session, a presentation, or a project. These are times of great anxiety for both the individual who is waiting for feedback and the people who are called on to give feedback.

The key is understanding that the task is enabling the individual to do his or her own reflection on his or her own presentation or project. This runs counter to the temptation to tell the person everything he or she did well and everything the person did not do so well. An environment that seeks to strengthen individuals seeks to deepen the individual's own capacity to reflect on his or her own performance.

Consequently, the coach's role, rather than giving specific feedback, is to occasion processing and reflection through specific questions. In addition to that, objective data may also be shared when the individual asks, "What questions did I actually ask?" or "How much time did I really take in this section?" or "During my presentation, what percentage of my time did I spend actually looking at the audience?"

DID YOU KNOW?

- The most important ingredient to this activity is not perfect performance but growing trust.
- When this activity is done well, people want to do it again.
- Listening well can help you grasp what crucial question to ask.

ACTIVITY

#41

Training, Coaching, or Project Feedback

Do this activity after a person has demonstrated a new skill, made a presentation, or completed a project. This activity is a conversation with the person who has just made the presentation. Here are four basic questions to ask.

1. WHAT WAS YOUR PLAN? or WHAT DID YOU INTEND TO DO? Even if this was talked about earlier, it is helpful to start at this safe point. Occasionally the original plan may have changed at the last moment because of new information. Consequently, hearing exactly what was intended can clarify things not understood in the presentation.

2. WHAT DO YOU SENSE CAME OFF WELL? or WHAT DO YOU THINK WORKED WELL? or WHAT PARTS WERE OF PARTICULARLY HIGH QUALITY? Again, please avoid the huge temptation to give your direct feedback. Your job is to foster the person's own critical thinking.

3. WHEN YOU DO THIS AGAIN, WHAT MIGHT YOU DO DIFFERENTLY? This immediately enables the person to engage in a thoughtful review, encouraging some self-reflection on ways to improve. The presupposition in this whole flow of questions is that insights which occur to people on their own mean more than someone else's "good ideas."

4. HOW CAN I HELP? or IN WHAT WAYS CAN WE ASSIST YOU? This continues to put the person in total control of the continuation of the coaching process.

Hints . . .

✓ This activity assumes it is possible for people to increase and deepen their capacity to assess their own performance. Furthermore it suggests that another person can assist in this just by asking questions.

✓ It may be helpful to take notes yourself during the presentation or report so that you have clear and objective information to share.

✓ Amazingly, when this is done in a style of encouragement and specificity, people grow in confidence and in appreciation for the opportunity to do their own thinking.

EXAMPLE

I led a two-day training for administrators, the focus of which was training in a structured method to carry out a participatory workshop. After experiencing the method and reviewing the steps and theory behind it, the group divided into teams to prepare to lead a portion of the workshop the next day in a role play situation.

After each person led a section of the full workshop, I paused to ask each one what he or she had done well. Responses were: "I was nervous at first but gradually became more confident." "My team prepared me well ahead of time." "I had everything written down in front of me so I didn't get confused." I then asked what they might do differently next time. People offered comments like: "Next time I will practice first in front of a mirror." "I would look people more directly in the eyes." "I would ask someone else to write on the chart paper because it is hard for me to write and concentrate at the same time." The encouraging style of the group and the nature of the questions permitted a nonthreatening atmosphere that fostered self-assessment.

#42

INDIVIDUAL
COMMITMENT

"There is a widely held myth that 'Personal is personal, and work is work, and never the twain shall meet.' But in actuality, 'personal' and 'work' are always integrally combined."
—Ritscher from Adams

Usage of People's Names

DESCRIPTION/BACKGROUND

Whenever possible during my facilitation, I try to use people's names in responding to them. The mood of the group shifts when names are used during the interaction. The group begins to congeal.

A name is one of the most personal aspects of an individual. Just as people respond almost immediately if they are called by the wrong name or if their name is misspelled or mispronounced, they also respond positively inside when they are addressed correctly. This is another way of acknowledging that you are working with unique individuals when you work with a group.

DID YOU KNOW?

• Hearing people's names creates an atmosphere of connection.

• People open up a little when their name is used.

• Our high-tech/high-touch environment has created a need for more appropriate informality rather than for stiffer formality.

ACTIVITY
#42 *Usage of People's Names*

This activity suggests the leader find ways such as name tags or name cards to make names available when they are not already known.

1. Although it may seem easier to use this technique with a small group you have been meeting with for a long time, no matter what the size or your familiarity with the group, it still requires discipline to make mention of names in the course of dialogue.

   "So, Tom, what you are saying is that the project you are recommending would benefit not only the clients but the company, too."

   "Mary, tell us a little more about what is involved with that."

2. Sometimes, a person speaks up in strong opposition to what most of the group has been saying. Instead of passing over the comment in an attempt to move on, I use such a comment as an opportunity to remind people that any group has many perspectives.

   "Note that from Stan's perspective, although this program would definitely increase revenue, the average cost per item does not warrant the expense. Let's hear another perspective."

   "What Joan said reminds us that when we suggested something like this last year, several other staff people voiced strong objections about it to the manager."

   "Steve is concerned that the employees are going to have a hard time buying in to this."

3. If I am working with a new group, during the introductory conversation, I make a little drawing of the table and fill in people's names as I hear them. This gives me another tool to refer to when I attempt to use a person's name.

Hints . . .

✓ One reason I repeat an opposing position with the person's name is to make sure the group hears the comment and also to make sure the individual knows that we have heard the comment. This way if a contrary decision is finally reached, the individual knows without a doubt that the opposing perspective was at least heard in the process of coming to another resolution of the issue.

✓ If this is your first time in front of a large group, I find name tags can be extremely helpful. As a person is speaking, I will glance at his or her name tag so that I can respond to the comment with the correct name.

✓ If the group is large, of course you will not be able to remember everyone's name. However, even if you use the names of only twenty percent of the group, it moves the group much closer to a feeling of familiarity and closeness and personal recognition. Even if you use only the names of the people who talk most frequently, the dynamic of using personal names has been established and is working in the group's favor.

EXAMPLE

Occasionally I am a little embarrassed when someone comes to me and says, "How do you remember everyone's name?" The truth is that most of the time I have not remembered them at all. I have used their name tags, I have used my chart, or I have only used the names of ten people out of the forty in the group. But the fact that the comment has been made communicates to me that my use of people's names has been noticed and has helped people feel recognized.

43

Things
That
Take
Effort

INDIVIDUAL COMMITMENT

" ... work is more than what you do to earn a paycheck; it involves personal commitment, personal satisfaction, and personal growth."
—Ritscher from Adams

Personalized Job Tools

DESCRIPTION/BACKGROUND

From time to time, or during a holiday, the facilitator may want to show concrete recognition of the team. Circumstances vary, of course, but one way this can be done is to give something that enhances people's sense of job professionalism.

Sometimes employees have a low self-image about their job or role. This can have a huge impact on employee morale. Consequently, personalized job tools which enhance that sense of professionalism have the possibility of increasing workers' self-image. Genuine experiences of self-worth increase individual commitment. A personalized job tool can help someone better perform his or her job, and it may also have the person's name on it.

DID YOU KNOW?

- Every time you use such a job tool, you are reminded of your connections to your work colleagues.
- An appropriate job tool can communicate, "I believe you are a professional just as I am."
- A personalized job tool can help to recreate a person's image of him- or herself.

ACTIVITY

#43 *Personalized Job Tools*

1. What you do in this area depends greatly on your own analysis of the group with which you are working. What you do also needs to fit your own personality. Ask yourself these questions:

   a. What is the mood of this group? How are people feeling about themselves? Has a particular project been giving the group a rough time?

   b. How are they feeling about what is going to happen next in their work?

   c. Is a recognition of the whole team needed more than individual recognition at the moment?

   d. What job tool can I offer that will encourage the individuals?

2. Answering some of these questions may help you discern what kind of concrete recognition would be most helpful for your group.

3. Possible personalized job tools include:

   a. Name plates for the desk

   b. Appointment books

   c. Note pads—"From Jim's desk. . . "

   d. Wall calendars

   e. Attractive pictures for wall space

Hints . . .

✓ I notice that many recognition items I hear about do not cost a lot of money. Yet, the impact is inestimable.

✓ Even an idea that sounds a little corny may be just the humorous item to perk up a group's spirit that is lagging or overburdened.

EXAMPLE

Recently a principal in New York state shared with me that as a holiday gift, he decided to give each staff member a personalized set of business cards. Many saw this as a genuine honoring of their professional status. Many had never had their own business cards before. Whether or not all of the staff used them, it communicated to them that the principal felt they were worthy of having such cards.

As part of an ongoing program of employee recognition, one company named an employee of the month and granted that person a parking space for the month near the front entrance. This costs absolutely no money but goes a long way toward building morale.

INDIVIDUAL
COMMITMENT

OCCASIONING INDIVIDUAL ACCOUNTABILITY/ABSOLUTION

INTRODUCTION TO ACCOUNTABILITY/ABSOLUTION

How do you enable people to sustain their motivation and commitment to work? In the past, the primary method involved threats and fear: "If you do not do this, that is what will happen." "You do it this way or you will lose your job or you will not get a raise." Such an environment encourages hiding the truth. In other words, if things are not going so well, you will not reveal that there is any problem at all. In this atmosphere, you present only the most glowingly positive facts and attempt to keep any other facts hidden from view.

In the supportive team environment, it is possible to share the truth. An uncompleted project, a failed experiment, a risk that has fallen flat on its face, a forgotten task—all of these can be acknowledged as well as successes and victories. The team knows it can only proceed successfully if the real situation is fully known. Once the facts are laid out on the table, the team can use its power to figure out how best to move next and to create the supportive actions that enable the entire team to move forward. The team does this first by demanding honesty and truth in its reporting, and second by pronouncing absolution on the situation as it is. That is why this training falls under individual commitment. Fear and threats reduce commitment; honesty and absolution increase commitment by

153

enabling the entire team to move forward. This creates an environment that beckons forth individual commitment and freely given energy for the task.

By further cementing the individuals to the team, this method enhances the environment for consensus. This atmosphere beckons the team to *want* to find the points of agreement. As the team interdependence and individual commitment grow, the foundation for deeper consensus is built.

#44

INDIVIDUAL
COMMITMENT

"By making and keeping promises to ourselves and others, little by little, our honor becomes greater than our moods." —Covey

Short Weekly Meetings

DESCRIPTION/BACKGROUND

Regular and short check-in meetings to discuss honestly what is happening are crucial to carrying out smooth implementation of projects. Getting the true picture out on the table provides a way to focus team energy not only on planning the next phase, but on how to resolve any particular unsolved issues or tasks.

When these meetings happen crisply and regularly, they deepen the team connection and therefore continue to enhance the possibility of more and more consensus across the team.

DID YOU KNOW?

- Many times we shy away from meeting with our colleagues because we fear we have not done enough.
- Short, consistent, regular meetings are a part of a weekly rhythm people can begin to anticipate positively.
- Short weekly meetings can be regarded as supports to getting work done rather than undesired interruptions to work flow.

ACTIVITY

#44 *Short Weekly Meetings*

1. A short context can help remind the team of the larger task of which it is a part; or perhaps you would want to mention the teams performing other parts of the task.

2. Next, each team member can honestly report about what has been accomplished in the previous week and what is left to be done.

3. Following all the reports, I suggest the insertion of some word of affirmation. A sentence that announces to the whole team the completion of the previous time period, an acknowledged receiving of all the accomplishments, as well as omissions or errors, provides the environment to move the team unencumbered into the future.

4. At this moment it is possible for the team to look at the next time period and perhaps make shifts in the task, in who is to do which task, and so on.

5. You can conclude with any brief announcements as well as a word on when the next meeting is. You may choose to end with some sentence or phrase that reminds people of the broader task, the deeper thing to which all are committed.

Hints . . .

✓ Step three may seem very awkward to perform for a while. I can only assure you that as that becomes more genuine, you set the stage for more truth to come to the team's attention. Furthermore, as stated earlier, you are beckoning forth deeper individual commitment.

✓ There is such a temptation when a task is not done to ask immediately, "Why didn't you get this done?" or "What is the matter with you?" Sometimes it is helpful to ask the person to say more about what has been going on to get more information. An accusatory question occasions a mood of defensiveness and calls for blaming someone else or withholding information. A request for more background information can lead you closer to the real implementation issue or block.

✓ Accountability or absolution assumes a team of responsible individuals.

EXAMPLE

LIST OF ABSOLUTIONS

1. The past week is over, and we are free to create the week to come.

2. This week has been difficult and trying. It is also finished. This week's victories and accomplishments beckon us forward.

3. Both our successes and failures are now part of the past. We are totally free to create the future.

4. We can release both our successes and our failures and now proceed unburdened to create the week to come.

5. This week, complete with our successes and struggles, now can inform us about how to do the tasks ahead.

6. (Go ahead, write your own absolution.)

_____

_____

For many years I belonged to an organization that demanded long hours and lots of energy for the tasks we had outlined for us. Weekly we met, frequently repeating sentences like the ones above. I believe the fact that we kept on doing this work year after year is related to our constantly articulating and re-articulating statements like these.

"With increasing turbulence, transience, and complexity in our society, both organizational and individual excellence will be at a premium." —Adams

"I Am Nervous About" Conversations

DESCRIPTION/BACKGROUND

Rather than accusing, blaming, and denying, the intent of this particular activity is to bring awareness to people's emotions and feelings about carrying out certain responsibilities. Some duties, tasks, or responsibilities occasion a lot of anxiety. It is possible to bring that anxiety into the open and lessen the control it has on people's behavior. This activity affirms that although many parts of our work are pleasing to us, each of us is required to do tasks that annoy us or make us nervous.

DID YOU KNOW?

- More people are anxious and nervous than we can imagine.
- Many times being anxious and nervous can reveal that people care about a task or project.
- There are some tasks about which it is very wise to be anxious.

ACTIVITY

#45   *"I Am Nervous About"* *Conversations*

1. Divide the group into pairs.

2. Ask each pair to discuss the following questions:

   a. What are you looking forward to in the implementation of this task?

   b. What are you fearful of, nervous about, or afraid of as you think of yourself carrying out this task?

   c. What are some gimmicks each of you have found helpful in carrying out tasks that cause a lot of anxiety?

   d. Some people use 3 x 5 cards to write themselves messages of encouragement. What message would you put on a 3 x 5 card to encourage yourself during this task?

3. Now that everyone has been through this conversation in pairs, you might ask each question of the total group and request that some share the answers they talked about in pairs.

4. If you do not have time for the whole-group discussion, you could ask a general question such as, "What did you talk about?" "What surprised you in your conversations?" or "What did you learn during your conversations?"

Hints . . .

✓ With a particularly astute group, you might even ask a deeper level question, for example, "Why did I decide to hold this kind of a conversation with you?"

✓ At every point you are trying to communicate that nervousness, anxiety, and tiredness are naturally a part of many tasks and activities. By talking about these openly, we indirectly pronounce an absolution over them, thereby freeing us to participate more calmly in the tasks at hand.

✓ The intent of all this is to increase individual involvement and commitment so that greater team cohesiveness will result in deeper levels of consensus and energy for the task.

EXAMPLE

After training a group in the kind of workshop methods I have been talking about in this book, the time approached when the group members were going to use these methods to lead community focus groups. It was clear to me that anxieties were running very high.

After pairing people, I asked a series of questions similar to the ones in this activity. Afterward I asked the whole group to volunteer some of the responses they had shared in pairs.

People seemed to be comforted that many others were expressing similar anxieties. Because of that they were better able to pay attention to those courageous individuals who were able to express hope and confidence in the midst of their anxieties.

INDIVIDUAL COMMITMENT

For The Committed

"The ultimate stage of involvement is the regular, spontaneous taking of initiative." —Peters

Implementation Learning Conversation

DESCRIPTION/BACKGROUND

A very indirect way of performing accountability and absolution is through a structured conversation that not only gets out the accomplishments and the struggles but also the learnings which have occurred to people as they have been carrying out their tasks.

This creates a new context for the efforts of the past time period. Usually people can only recall how tough it has been or the failures they have had. Pulling out of the experience some gems of learning and insight can wrap the difficult experience in a new light, which can free the group to move into the next time period with more hope and confidence.

DID YOU KNOW?

- Even disasters have hidden learnings.
- People grow more proficient when you take a moment to talk about their learnings.
- Many learnings do not reveal themselves until called forth in the midst of intentional conversation.

ACTIVITY

#46 *Implementation Learning Conversation*

This conversation best happens at the conclusion of a natural time period or at the completion of a project. This is most effective when everyone on the team is present. Proceed from question to question with the group, after the group has given four or five responses to each question.

1. In the past quarter, what have been some of our key accomplishments and victories?

2. What are some things that worked well for us?

3. What were some of our hardest struggles?

4. What were some failures?

5. How are we in a different position than we were three months ago?

6. What are some learnings we have had through the activities we have implemented in these past three months?

7. What changes can we suggest now for how we go about things in the next three months?

8. What title shall we give these past three months? (e.g., "The Great Quarter of _____ .")

Hints . . .

✓ The value of a conversation such as this is that it is carried out totally from a team perspective. No one person's accomplishments or failures are highlighted. This provides one form of accountability and absolution.

✓ The assumption of this conversation is that even our failures teach us something valuable and can assist us in the future.

✓ This in no way suggests that there are no longer any differences. When differences arise, the individually committed team members want to work hard at finding a solution that will work and satisfy the perspectives and values represented.

✓ A slight modification of this conversation could be used to help an individual get perspective on something that did not turn out well. The flow of these questions can also be used to help people step back and process a disaster.

✓ This, of course, is not a weekly conversation. However, it could easily be a regular quarterly one.

EXAMPLE

After leading this entire conversation with several teams, here are some of the implementation learnings people shared with their teams:

1. Successful implementation increases team and individual confidence.
2. Successful implementation sparks other successes.
3. A well-chosen project can transform the mood of an entire organization.
4. Success invites others on board.
5. Finding ways to keep regularly connected with the other teams is crucial.
6. We need some work as a whole group to map out how we intend to make decisions together.

*"Involvement can start with
anything. Maybe even a party."*
—Peters

A Victory Party
Before the Victory

DESCRIPTION/BACKGROUND

It is not uncommon to hold a victory celebration after a task is
completed. In addition to a party or a meal, I have also held brief
conversations rehearsing various things that happened in the victory
and asking about the implications of the victory.

However, this particular activity suggests holding a victory
celebration *before* the event. In other words, you are using such an
event to project everyone into a winning spirit before the victory
occurs. You are proclaiming with confidence that there is no way
that your team can lose. This is a bold claim. It acknowledges ahead
of time that not everything will go perfectly. It also declares ahead of
time that the plan has been created with victory built into it. It
proclaims that no matter what the mistakes may be in implementation, it is failure-proof.

This is a radical declaration of absolution that takes everyone's
fears and worries and sets them into a place of victory.

DID YOU KNOW?

- A victory party before the victory communicates that the group will discern a
  victory whether it occurs or not.
- Everyone wants to be part of a winning team—the wise leader helps
  everyone see they are winners.

A C T I V I T Y

#47 *A Victory Party Before the Victory*

This activity suggests doing something confident and maybe a little outrageous before your task is completed: declaring your victory before you have won.

1. As the leader, pay attention to the mood of your group.

2. If anxieties are running high about a particularly critical project or event ask, "What could we do to celebrate ahead of time our confidence that we are going to win at this?"

3. Make a list of the suggestions from the group on chart paper. Some possibilities could be: going out to dinner, going to a movie, or having refreshments at the next meeting.

4. Talk for a minute about the values of each possibility and what each one communicates.

5. Choose one and set a time.

6. Quickly divide up the responsibilities.

Hints . . .

✓ The key is to let the group put the particulars together.

✓ Even the whole mood of a victory celebration before the victory may come as very offensive to hard-liner types. This kind of event cannot be forced.

✓ Let the group members declare the meaning of the event. Once you have raised the idea, let them decide the significance of doing this. Such meaning cannot be preached at the group.

EXAMPLE

I was part of the training of a dozen facilitators who were about to begin two full weeks of leading workshops they had never led before. Furthermore, a lot was riding on the success of these two weeks. The night before the workshops began all the newly trained facilitators, their bosses, and the trainers gathered for a victory celebration.

We used a few moments during the party to state in a group conversation exactly what victories we were hoping for. We also spent time imagining the new position the organization would be in if all worked out well.

Needless to say, on the last day we went out to dinner to hold a "victory after the fact" celebration.

"Indeed, it could be argued that a 'critical mass' of individual members need to undergo personal transformations before their organizations can undergo system-wide transformation."
—Adams

Symbol of Commitment

DESCRIPTION/BACKGROUND

Some groups have discerned ways to create symbols of their individual commitments to the task and to their team. This is another activity that best occurs out of the spontaneous decisions of the team. When it does happen, it can be very powerful in crystallizing a group's decision to work together. These symbols can be very concrete reminders to everyone of their decisions to work together as a team to accomplish their goal or project.

DID YOU KNOW?

- Participating in an appropriate symbol of commitment can be a deeply binding rite of passage.
- An appropriate symbol for one group of people may not call forth any commitment for a different group—i.e., genuine symbols are very group-specific.
- A wise leader stays alert for unexpected appearances of such symbols.

ACTIVITY

#48 *Symbol of Commitment*

After a group has been meeting for a while, or after a group has just experienced a real change in how it is organized or a dramatic shift in some of its responsibilities, sometimes it decides to create some kind of symbol of its intention to carry this through to the end.

The following conversation might help the group formalize its commitment.

1. What are some of the changes we are experiencing lately?

2. How are these changes altering us as a group?

3. How would you talk about the way our commitment to our task is deepening?

4. What object or symbol could we create to remind us of our commitment? (Perhaps a common team notebook for each person, a visual symbol on the inside of a notebook, or a sentence.)

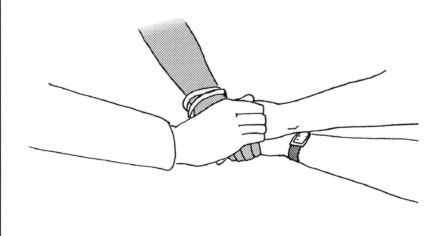

Hints . . .

✓ **The power of this activity is in its spontaneity.**

✓ **The leader's skill is required in noticing when these symbols have emerged in the life of the team.**

✓ **Even humorous symbols can represent serious commitment.**

EXAMPLE

I worked with a staff who had been experiencing a great deal of back-biting and gossip. After an intensive two days of creating plans for the next phase of organizational growth, the team responsible for effective leadership stood up and declared that the following week, each person would be requested to sign a team oath. Within a few days, this team had created a professional looking small certificate stating: "I,_____, vow with all my professional ethics and promise to never speak ill or in a derogatory manner against another staff member." Each person signed it. At the same time, the team suggested that if there was any issue or concern about an individual's professional behavior it would be given to the effective leadership team and then not talked about again from that point on. In this situation it worked. The planning focus and the signed oath united the group to work professionally in a way this staff had not seen in two or three years.

170

COLLABORATIVE
TEAMS

"The power of self-managing teams has been demonstrated in numerous settings. Why do they work? Quite simply, people of groups of ten to thirty can get to know one another well, can learn virtually every one else's tasks, can be gotten together with little fuss, and under enlightened leadership can readily achieve unit cohesion and esprit." (Peters, 1987, p. 302)

Team synergy calls for the team-building skills that can move a team in the direction of consensus. Teams do not just happen. There are many ways the parts can act together. Most of us have many experiences of groups of people who have no knowledge or capacity for acting together. Leadership skills and openness are required. Likewise, consensus does not just happen. People who have been trained in rugged individualism and in confrontational modes of operating cannot suddenly overnight become smooth-operating teams facile at creating consensus.

Just getting people to sit around a table together does not guarantee a smooth working team. Indeed, Blake et al. (1987) refers to the potential of either "positive collectivity" or "negative collectivity." When a positive collectivity is created, the way is paved for authentic consensus. The connections and links made between

171

individuals open up the potential for consensus. The deeper the team connection, the greater the potential for consensus.

Team synergy emerges with a skillful combination of focus on the external team task as well as the trust and nurture among the team members. Single-minded drive toward the team task soon leads to burnout or robotic accomplishment of duties. Warmth and mutual support in a vacuum soon turn sterile when enclosed in a self-serving group. Synergy is the product of deep human connections joined in accomplishing a common task.

"Valuing the differences is the essence of synergy—the mental, the emotional, the psychological differences between people" (Covey, 1990, p. 277). The heart of team synergy is discovering the value of the differences that exist in the team. When the positive value of the individual differences is embraced, then the capacity to build consensus increases. At the same time, the team cohesiveness and the team energy expand.

Operating in teams is a totally different mode of working than either the top-down, decision-making mode chief executive officers have used or the instructional mode teachers have utilized. Both the teacher and the chief executive officer have been the primary focus of information in those old modes. Today, the style of the facilitator presupposes that much knowledge exists already among the workers in the organization. Calling it forth, building on it, extending it beyond what is already known demands new skills of operating. What is at stake here is effectiveness. The old modes no longer work.

Peter Senge (1990) gives us a clue as to what kinds of skills are needed. Some skills enable a group to get out as many ideas as possible. These skills enable a group to see the perspective of a variety of available options. These options can get out on the table relatively quickly with little or no evaluation or judgment applied to them. Once that has occurred then you need methods to enable a group to narrow the options down to a workable number. Finally, you need methods that help a group to decide which options it will go with. These are not methods that have been taught to a society much more accustomed to top-down decision making or confrontational battles during which the loudest or strongest win.

Senge suggests that once a group is formed, it is possible to access a level of thinking built out of the individual minds represented in the group that is greater than the power of each of the individual minds. In the best sense of the word, I suggest Senge is pointing to the mind of the whole group. This "group mind" is decidedly opposite from the term "group think" which refers to a mindset where everyone in a group thinks and operates the same way. The group mind as I refer to it is a mind made up of many strong individual minds with distinct independent thought. These minds are bound together for a common end. That very bonding has created a distinct product: the group mind. Methods and tools to access this group mind can call forth creativity, alternative options, and solutions that one mind alone would have trouble generating.

Senge points the way to an additional potential in a bonded team—that of stepping back from the task and reflecting on what is going on in order to derive learnings and meanings. The skill to do that cannot only call forth critical insights for the carrying out of the task but can also create deeper bonds among the members of the team, bonds that can exponentially increase the capacity for deeper and deeper consensus.

The excitement of team accomplishment and team diversity drives the journey toward consensus. According to Covey (1990), it is critical to see excitement for the team accomplishment and inter-dependence as a developmental step way beyond mere dependence on other people to get your job done for you. A fine-tuned instrument is in the process of growing and maturing. As the team members take delight in their own accomplishments and in their own life together, the sense of team reaches new depths. The connections are tighter. Challenges are looked forward to, not run away from and dreaded. Through interdependence, a powerful, effective, dynamic force is constantly being recreated.

When teams have come to this stage of development, each team member has come to realize that the strength of the team is built on the different gifts each person brings to the team. In other words, the power of the team is in its diversity. (Again, this is very different from the creation of a team of robots symbolized in group think modes.) It is because of this deep valuing of diversity, honoring the differences in perspectives, and welcoming of different viewpoints that consensus is enhanced. Differences are welcomed, even trusted. When this happens new levels of consensus now open up as walls of distrust come down.

When teams function well and operate out of consensus in their decision making, the result is visible accomplishment. Team members are enthusiastic about their work and ready for the next challenge.

173

Teams living out of consensus and action are what will make the difference. The demand is overwhelming, for it calls for a way of operating we may find strange. Yet the evidence is in. Not only does it all work, but it is possible to have it all happen in a way that makes this very work something we want to participate in. Work has the possibility of once again generating our excitement and enthusiasm. Consensus is the vital process to making that possibility a reality.

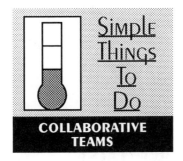

INTENSIFYING
TEAM IDENTITY

INTRODUCTION TO TEAM IDENTITY

Western society has operated over recent time with an emphasis on
the individual. Responsibility and accountability occurred person by
person. Now, however, particularly with the corporate world discovering the effectiveness of teamwork, collaboration is demanded in the
work place. Although individual accountability is always a critical
component, communication skills and the ability to work coopera-
tively are sought more and more. Yet, for many of us, operating in
teams comes as a brand new experience, fraught with challenges and
pitfalls along with promises.

Teams increase their effectiveness as their identity is enhanced. A
team is an organism—an entity, just as an individual is an organism.
Affirming and nurturing this organism increases its productivity.
Acknowledging the presence of teams almost needs to be overempha-
sized to successfully counter our accustomed ways of operating as
individuals. Creating the bond of team dramatizes to its members
another way of operating.

Consensus building is about creating trust and making connections
among people. The team, by fostering a sense of identity outside of
the individual, inculcates a possibility of relatedness and trust that is
foundational to efforts toward consensus. The more successfully
teams can connect with each other and interact, the more potential
there is for genuine consensus.

175

Simple
Things
To
Do
**COLLABORATIVE
TEAMS**

"Teamwork is a plural process. It cannot be done by one person." —Blake, Mouton, and Allen

Team Member List

DESCRIPTION/BACKGROUND

Listing the teams and the team members is foundational. It is a declaration of how things are going to operate. In the past, teams have been primarily advisory. In shared decision making, teams are for implementation. Some recommendations and/or decisions will be popular, and some will be disliked. A list of team members makes visible the mechanism now operating for coming up with recommendations, decisions, and implementation.

Naming the team members gives the broader group access to what is going on. A worker might be reluctant to ask the manager about a particular issue. On the other hand, this same worker having a coffee break might talk more easily to his or her fellow worker on the appropriate team.

This list of team members is the new organizational chart. It may be a little oversimplified, but this list could symbolize that now the recommendations, decisions, and accountability lie with the teams. In addition, this is a tool that communicates the importance of every individual to the life and success of the team.

DID YOU KNOW?

- A list of team members communicates that everyone is needed for the accomplishment of the group task.
- Keeping the list up to date communicates that teams are vital to the success of the group.

ACTIVITY
#49   *Team Member List*

1. Print a list of all team members, using their full names spelled correctly.

2. Make sure that everyone on the team receives a copy of the list.

3. Make sure this list is posted in the meeting room area and in a central area for all to see.

4. As changes occur, update the list.

5. Use this list as a way to check who is there for the team meeting.

Hints . . .

✓ The radical nature of the team member list can become apparent when the first controversial decision needs to be made. In the past we have named the manager to be the one to both make the decision and take the praise or blame. We are suggesting that recommendations come from the teams and be reviewed by the whole group or a representative body.

✓ Many managers may want to rescue their teams from controversy or even outright hostility. The much trickier role for the manager is to make sure each team has all the necessary data to make an informed decision. Then it is time to step back and allow the consequences to shared decision making—both the uplifting ones and the struggles—to unfold.

EXAMPLE

When I lead a planning session, we usually move into the implementation planning that is always done by teams after doing several sessions of whole group planning. As we prepare the entire planning document, I make sure the list of who is on which team is included. This is part of what can remain long after I am gone.

To ease into this mode of operating, some groups I have worked with suggest that every person be on at least one team—but of their own choosing. This blends elements of assignment and choice. The team list communicates to the group that shared decision making is to continue from that point on.

#50

"Dependent people need others to get what they want. Independent people can get what they want through their own effort. Interdependent people combine their own efforts with the efforts of others to achieve their greatest success." —Covey

Team Name

DESCRIPTION/BACKGROUND

After the team has worked a short while together, finding a team name is one way to encourage team identity. Naming the team becomes a way to assume ownership of this team, of acknowledging that each person is now part of a group accountable for a specific task. The name may be somehow related to the team task, in which case it solidifies the members in their team focus. Otherwise, the name may represent a quality or characteristic that the members want their team to embody.

DID YOU KNOW?

- The team name can remind each team member of his or her connection with the others on the team.
- The team name formally identifies this new team organism.
- The team name can communicate the team's unique gifts and personality.

A C T I V I T Y

#50　*Team Name*

1. Clarify who the members of each team are. Make sure that everyone has been placed on a team.

2. After the teams have done some planning together so that individuals have had some initial contact with each other, have each team return to the team work space for five minutes to come up with a team name.

3. Suggest to the group that the name might come out of the particular team's assigned responsibility or out of the personalities or skills of the members.

4. After each team has chosen a name, bring all the teams back together to hear team reports.

5. Clap for or acknowledge each team name.

6. Process the activity by asking:

    a. "How did your team work together to choose its name?"

    b. "As all of these names were announced, what did you hear or what did you think about?"

    c. "What has happened to us through this team naming process?"

Hints . . .

✓ There is an added impact to this naming process when a larger group breaks up into teams to create each team's name. When you bring the total group together and hear the team names, it creates a lot of momentum and spirit.

✓ It does not necessarily take a long time to find a team name. It might be helpful to couple the choosing of a team name with one of the other team identity activities listed in this section. This will enhance the creativity.

EXAMPLE

Sometimes a particular theme for the year or a theme of a recent talk by someone inspires a team name. In one organization, the director had given a fine talk on how well geese work together as teams. During that talk, he mentioned that geese behind the lead goose often honk as a way to encourage the leader to keep on. Sure enough, when teams met to choose their names, one team chose the name "Honkers" to symbolize how they wanted to keep encouraging each other and all of the teams in their tasks. I liked that name because every time they hear it, they will remember not only their assigned task but the style they wish to use as they carry out the task.

Another team created a name out of the first two letters of each of the team members' names. In other words, Sue, Mary, Jane, and Marilyn became the SUMAJAMA team!

Simple
Things
To
Do
COLLABORATIVE TEAMS

> *"The key issue is in how the parts act together—participation. It is the core issue of productivity, creativity, and satisfaction."*
> —Blake, Mouton, and Allen

Team Flag or Symbol

DESCRIPTION/BACKGROUND

Choosing the team name in the previous activity drew on the verbal intelligence of the group. Translating the identity of the group into a visual symbol or a flag draws on the visual/spatial intelligence of the group, thus cementing its identity in an additional mode.

Once a flag or other team symbol is created, it can become a permanent part of the team meeting area. The team flag or symbol can capture visually what that team wants to be about.

This can also be a tool to remind the team members of the big picture—the reason why they are carrying out very mundane daily tasks. A quick glance at the visual symbol can tie a person into the original purpose or goal for his or her work.

DID YOU KNOW?

- A team flag or banner proudly and blatantly proclaims the greatness of the team to its fellow group members and colleagues.
- A team flag can include unique aspects of that particular team's task or focus.
- Displaying the team flag can remind people of the significance of the team's task better than words can.

ACTIVITY

#51 *Team Flag or Symbol*

1. Ahead of time, gather appropriate materials to assist the teams in this activity, such as chart paper or poster board, markers, and masking tape.

2. Give each team ten or fifteen minutes to create its visual symbol or flag.

3. Tell them ahead of time to choose a reporter. (This will alert them to the reporting time and remind them that each team will be "on stage.")

4. Walk around and note the progress as a way to judge how much more time may be needed on this activity.

5. During the reports, have each team remind the larger group of its own team name before describing its symbol or flag.

6. Appropriately acknowledge each presentation.

7. At the conclusion of the entire presentation, enable the group to step back and process the whole experience with one or two of these questions:

   a. What was easy about this?

   b. What was hard about this?

   c. Which flags particularly caught your attention?

   d. As you look at all these flags, what message(s) are they communicating?

   e. What did you learn about your group as you did this?

Hints . . .

✓ **Identity does not just happen. It needs direct encouragement. Perhaps some people have never really worked on a team before. Therefore, tools to enhance identity need to be included in the overall flow of the work of the team.**

✓ **Encourage each team to be as visual as possible.**

✓ **Some teams really build on this work. It can become a genuine source of identification.**

EXAMPLE

When I worked with many schools from one small city, the team that came from the northern part of the city named itself the Northern Stars and among other things put stars in their symbol. A team of math and science teachers put some science and math symbols on its flag.

Some of the flags became very elaborate, almost works of art. Motivation went sky-high after this reporting and sharing time.

"The whole is greater than the sum of its parts. The team result has exceeded the sum of individual contribution; that's the meaning of excellence in teamwork when teamwork becomes spectacular." —Blake, Mouton, and Allen

Team Motto

DESCRIPTION/BACKGROUND

A motto or slogan is a further piece of identification for a team. A short phrase or sentence can hold some crucial part of the team task or summarize the team's hopes and visions.

The nature of a motto or slogan is upbeat. No one writes a depressing motto. In this activity, you are providing a vehicle for affirmative team spirit to be declared. The very process of choosing a team motto helps the team focus, through the power of language, the unique essence of that team's spirit.

DID YOU KNOW?

- A team motto can capture in a few words just what that team is all about.
- A team motto, which can be remembered during times of stress and difficulty, can provide just the right motivation to keep the team going until the task is finished.
- A short, well-written team motto is hard to forget.

ACTIVITY

#52　　*Team Motto*

1. Have some possible mottos or slogans at your fingertips to use as examples. Have people suggest catchy slogans from companies or advertisements.

2. Give each team five minutes to come up with their own motto or slogan.

3. Have each team assign a reporter who will share the motto with everyone.

4. After each team is finished, call on the reporters to share the mottos with the whole group.

5. At the end, process the experience with one or two of these questions:

    a. Which word or phrase do you remember?

    b. Which one(s) do you like?

    c. What are some of the important themes communicated by these mottos and slogans?

Hints . . .

✓ Since a lot of the value of these team-identity vehicles is ongoing, creating ways to keep these names, flags, and mottos in front of everyone can further increase their power. Everyone is encouraged and empowered by all the teams' creativity and spirit.

✓ As you can see, each one of these activities does not need to take a long time. By spending just ten minutes out of a ninety-minute meeting, you generate a great deal of spirit. This helps to create a difference between a boring committee meeting and a lively team meeting that can actually leave you refreshed and motivated.

EXAMPLE

In my recent work with science and math teachers, I have seen some national organizations create the slogan "Science matters. Math counts." I know I will remember that slogan for a long time. Furthermore, it reminds me of the crucial role of science and math.

The Northern Stars team mentioned earlier created the slogan "The stars will shine." That slogan could communicate that these people intend to carry out activities that will be noticed. Another team's slogan is "Every kid's a winner with us." To me this communicates the hope that every student's gifts can be discovered and released.

"Only when concern for a team result is integrated with trust and mutual support among members is synergy likely to emerge."
—Blake, Mouton, and Allen

Team Song

DESCRIPTION/BACKGROUND

In a relatively short time, you can lead a team in writing its own team song. By choosing a melody and doing a short brainstorm on the history, role, or qualities of your team, you can prepare the ingredients for a song. Tapping the creativity of the whole team can produce the words to fit the melody. The song can be just one verse, one verse and a chorus, or even several verses.

We already know that songs can communicate feelings and commitment in a way that words miss. A team song can tap the power of poetry and the spirit of music and infuse them into the team experience. Just as with the slogan, it is really hard to write a negative song about your team. A song can celebrate both the importance of the team task and the appreciation of the teammates for each other as they have been working together.

DID YOU KNOW?

- A team song can be written even if you are not good in music.
- A team song holds power to connect that plain words cannot.
- When team songs are heard by others they occasion great appreciation for the creativity of the team.

ACTIVITY
#53　*Team Song*

1. Give people the choice of composing a song, rap, or team cheer. This activity should take about twenty minutes.

2. Brainstorm ideas and phrases that tell how the team has worked together. This is a good time to mention some of the group's recent accomplishments.

3. Then, brainstorm on paper some tunes that people know well, are fairly singable, and are upbeat.

4. Once you have listed several tunes, have the group pick one to work with.

5. When the tune has been picked, work with the group to "line out" the song. Lining out a song means drawing a short line for every syllable of the words to that song.

   For example,

   YAN KEE DOO DLE CAME TO TOWN is seven syllables.

   ___ ___ ___ ___ ___ ___ ___

6. After you have lined the verse, ask, "How shall we start?"

7. Gradually people will fill in the lines with words and phrases, using some of the ideas from the brainstorm and others that just occur to them.

8. Changes and revisions will be made continually.

9. When a verse is done, have the team sing it through to see how it sounds. This will create further revisions, perhaps, or inspire the team to write another verse.

10. Listening to the songs other teams have written really raises the mood of the teams.

11. As each team sings its song, applaud or recognize each team for its creativity.

12. Ask one or two processing questions at the end:

   a. What did you like about this?

   b. What insights came to you as you were writing your song?

   c. What did you discover about yourself or your team as you wrote your song?

13. Later, have the teams sing their songs or even add new verses.

Hints . . .

✓ **This activity works well with a group of people who have worked together for a while. You might do this two or three months after the team has been formed. This will not work with a group that feels that singing is a waste of time. Many people do not like to sing or feel it is silly for a work team to engage in singing. Many cultures, however, have realized the value of a song for focusing the energies of people for work.**

✓ **When a team seems to be stuck on an issue or a problem, having the team sing its song can often break the thinking loose.**

EXAMPLE

I was invited back to Appleton, Wisconsin, to work with a number of teachers and business people on their "Partnership Projects"—an effort to create business-education partnerships in Appleton. Since it was the second year I had worked with them, I decided to have part of the group create a song and another part of the group create a story. After a time together to brainstorm what might go into both, this is what the song group created to the tune of "Hey, Look Me Over":

> Hey, look us over
> See what we've done
> We've got ideas and
> It's been lots of fun.

To help our Valley grow
Businesses and schools
And parents and kids
We're all a part of
The show . . . .

AND NOW IT'S

On to the future
There's lots that we can do
Shadowing and sharing
There's always something new
Partnership Projects
have started us moving
So come let's get the job done
We're the future

WE ARE ONE!

#54

"Life is, by nature, highly interdependent. To try to achieve maximum effectiveness through independence is like trying to play tennis with a gold club—the tool is not suited to the reality. Interdependence is a far more mature, more advanced concept." —Covey

Team Rituals or Rites

DESCRIPTION/BACKGROUND

There are simple rites and rituals that just emerge in the life of the team. The leader may not plan for them; often they just happen. And then the wise leader lets them grow.

Sometimes it is a word, phrase, or something which happened to one of the team members that gets repeated again and again in similar team situations. All of these help a team to create its own identity, making it a distinct group among all the other teams.

DID YOU KNOW?

- Some of the best team rituals and rites appear naturally and unexpectedly rather than during a team session to create one.
- Team rituals and rites often emerge after a sudden team breakthrough or victory.
- Because team rituals and rites are often linked with victory or breakthrough, they can motivate the team by indirectly reminding them of the victory and breakthrough.

ACTIVITY

#54 *Team Rituals or Rites*

This activity is out to foster gestures, phrases, or objects that take on a unique and special role in the life of a team and help to claim its identity to each team member.

1. As these rituals or rites often appear without warning, there is no substitute for keeping alert for their occurrences.

2. Your very relaxed and open style as a leader-facilitator can help to encourage such rituals or rites to emerge.

3. If you experience a team success or project breakthrough, you can capitalize on the sense of accomplishment or victory by asking, "What gesture or phrase could capture how we are feeling right now?" or "What gesture or phrase would congratulate us all for this job well done?"

4. Watch the dialogue. If this idea catches on, let the team try to come up with something.

5. If not, verbally congratulate the team and suggest that maybe at another time a ritual or rite might emerge.

Hints . . .

✓ Some teams meet every week or two just to celebrate their victories. Maybe it is over coffee. Maybe they have breakfast together or they go out for lunch.

✓ Rituals and rites may seem to take time away from carrying out a task. In reality they are keeping people's motivation and performance ability high. The wise leader is pleased when such things grow.

EXAMPLE

One team I have worked with has created a gesture—all slapping their hands together in the center of the table when they have completed their task. No other team has done that. It belongs uniquely to that team and bonds the members together every time they use it.

Another team had a "cynic jar" in the center of the table. Whenever anyone made a cynical comment or cut off an idea at the start, that person deposited a nickel in the jar. This was a rite that team created very naturally to foster encouragement and to bring awareness to unhelpful and cynical comments.

COLLABORATIVE
TEAMS

INCREASING SUPPORTIVE CONNECTION

INTRODUCTION TO CONNECTION

Connection has to do with the ties people on the team sense between themselves. People who feel connected can say one or more of the following sentences: "When I speak, I am understood. My ideas make sense to others on the team." "If I am having difficulty carrying something out, I can get some supportive suggestions." "When I run into an unexpected additional work assignment, I can turn to the people on the team for some concrete assistance." "I am ready to offer help to teammates when a personal issue prevents them from finishing a task." "I always check a new idea out with a member of the team." This kind of deep connecting emerges as the trust among teammates continues to grow.

A collaborative team needs not only a strong team identity but also individuals who are connected to each other, who in their work interact and interrelate with each other. They grow in knowing that they can trust their teammates. They learn to depend on each other. This sense of connection does not happen automatically and never gets much of a start in some teams.

Genuine connection thus becomes one of the critical ingredients for authentic consensus. Because genuine connection takes a while to emerge, it reveals why true consensus does not just happen overnight with a group pulled together for the first time. The more serious the issue needing consensus, the more there needs to be some sense of connection.

195

COLLABORATIVE
TEAMS

"When people come together to form groups, each member brings a personal set of knowledge, skills, values, and motivations. How these interact to form a collectivity can be positive or negative." —Blake, Mouton, and Allen

Winning Team Story

DESCRIPTION/BACKGROUND

Every individual as well as every team possesses a conscious or unconscious story. This activity brings awareness of a team's story and indeed enables the team to live and work out of a winning team story. This activity guides the team to the writing of its own story.

Marty Seldman's book, *Self-Talk: The Winning Edge in Selling*, reminds us of the role of individual self-talk relative to an individual's performance at selling. His insight goes much further than selling and the individual: "What we believe and say to ourselves quickly and strongly influences our feelings and actions" (Seldman, 1986, p. 10). A team's spoken or unspoken story about itself, written or unwritten story about itself, can have a direct impact on its own performance.

This activity brings to awareness and visibility a team story that will continue over time to increase its effective performance by strengthening its sense of connection.

DID YOU KNOW?

- A winning team story reminds people when the going gets rough of past victories and future hopes.
- A winning team story sets the present moment into a much broader picture.
- Individuals need to be reminded that they are part of a winning team even though their particular tasks might be going poorly.

ACTIVITY

#55 *Winning Team Story*

1. Set out materials such as chart paper, markers, masking tape, pencil, and paper.

2. Set the stage by saying a few words about the role of winning stories. You might ask the group:

   a. What successful teams have you been a part of?

   b. What do you imagine were the stories these teams had about themselves that helped them to win?

3. Brainstorm with the whole group ideas under each of these three areas:

The Past	The Present	The Future
What has happened	What is going on now	Where we want to be
Our past accomplishments	Our current challenges	Future victories

4. Divide the whole group into three teams, one to work on each of the above three sections.

5. Have the teams take ten to fifteen minutes to pull together a paragraph on their assigned section. You might suggest they write their paragraphs onto chart paper. Then it will be easy to display to the whole group.

6. Have representatives from each team read the paragraph until all three sections have been heard.

7. Applaud after the whole story has been read.

8. End with some processing questions:

   a. What words or phrases do you remember from our story?

   b. What parts of the story did you like best?

   c. What does the story communicate about what kind of team we are?

   d. What do you think we should do with this story?

Hints . . .

✓ **This activity can be done in conjunction with writing the team song (see Activity #53).**

✓ **You might decide to get this story printed up and distributed to everyone in the group. Every so often having this story read could remind people in a positive and indirect way why that team exists and why they are connected to each other.**

EXAMPLE

A group I worked with in Wisconsin was creating business-education partnerships between local businesses and the local schools. The members of this group called themselves Partnership Projects. After the first year of implementation, when I returned for a second conference, the group wrote this story about its work and its role.

PROGRESS IN ACTION — NEW HORIZONS

Our Community Situation

Once upon a time, an energetic and growing city, located on the banks of the Fox River, was given the challenge of improving its stature.

The community recognized its shortcomings. Foremost in its concern were the few children not succeeding. Some of the children were not acquiring a work ethic, some were deficient in basic skills, some were dropping out of school . . . some weren't developing to their best potentials.

The community saw a need for a change . . . a new breath of fresh air. Business and education alike saw this need and recognized that business was largely an untapped resource in the public schools. A mutual team effort was seen as a solution to benefit business, education, community, and children alike.

Our First Year's Accomplishments

In A.D. 1986 the first Partnership Conference was held. From that conference needs were identified and ideas sprang forth.

It came to pass that a logo was established giving momentum to the partnership project.

Great feasts took place with gourmet luncheons. Awareness was expanded with career festivals, the updating of the tour guides, and the creation of a speakers bureau. Jobs were shadowed. Presentations were made to teachers. The National Symposium was attended and Partnership Conference II has brought visions of lasting significance to the year's work.

So it is said, so it shall be.

Our Hopes and Dreams

It is our vision to unify the small as well as the large businesses with the educational system to bring to our young people the promise of a better future. A future that includes an awareness of their own capabilities and how they may be contributing members of the society; to feel useful, productive, and most of all, needed in the community.

#56

"The modest-sized, task-oriented, semi-autonomous, mainly self-managing team should be the basic organization building block." —Peters

Leadership Rotation

DESCRIPTION/BACKGROUND

All the roles necessary for leading and supporting the meeting can be rotated and shared among the team members. The upfront leader, the person who gets the room set up and ready, the person who takes notes on the meeting, the person who brings coffee or a snack, the person who cleans up after the meeting—all these roles can be named and a rotation system prepared to share these responsibilities.

This is a great way to train everyone in assuming responsibility for various aspects of the life of the team. If, for example, the person assigned to be the facilitator-leader for a meeting does not know how methodologically to lead a portion of the meeting, this is an opportunity for that person to be trained.

There are some people who have great difficulty with rotation. If you can pull it off, it does demonstrate a lateral team structure as compared to our traditional hierarchical ways of carrying out responsibilities.

Not only does this method train people, but also it allows everyone's unique approaches and gifts to be utilized. Personally, if I am not assigned to do something, I am reluctant to put myself in any kind of major leading role.

Furthermore, this demonstrates that the person who may traditionally be thought of as the leader is willing to set up the room, to provide the refreshments, and to clean up and wash the dishes. This communicates in powerful ways that no one ever "graduates" out of the nitty-gritty tasks that help pull off an event.

DID YOU KNOW?

- Leadership rotation communicates the trust of the group in each other's competence.
- Leadership rotation reveals hidden talents.
- Leadership rotation continues to renew the energy of the team.

ACTIVITY

#56 *Leadership Rotation*

This activity enables the team to create its own leadership rotation chart. Although one person could draw this up, creating this as a team activity fosters more buy-in.

1. Set a context that each person can do any role.

2. Brainstorm the various roles and tasks necessary for a meeting (e.g., room set-up, leader, secretary, report writer, room clean-up, refreshments).

3. List those down the left side of a piece of chart paper.

4. List the next eight to ten meeting dates across the top.

5. Have the group decide how to fill in the slots (e.g., random rotation, sign-up).

6. Print this and distribute it to everyone at the next meeting.

7. Suggest that if any conflicts or difficulties arise, it is the individual's responsibility to make switches or changes.

8. Clarify who people can check with should they have any questions on how to carry out their assigned role for any given meeting.

Hints . . .

✓ **If certain people resist strongly, work around them. These alternating responsibilities are opportunities, not hard and fast rules.**

✓ **Another way to divide up assignments is to divide your group of ten into three subteams and assign the responsibilities on a meeting basis to the subteams. If one person does not feel able to carry out a responsibility, the subteam will deal with it, either by encouraging that person to go ahead or putting another person up for the role who is open to carrying it out.**

✓ **This entails some clear write-ups on what the various responsibilities are and how to carry them out.**

EXAMPLE

In an organization I once worked for, my real training happened in a smaller team where every week assignments for different duties and responsibilities were rotated. In an effective team where connections are strong and positive, those who have been around a while are eager to assist you in your preparation.

The various rotating roles included getting notices out about the coming meeting, leading an opening conversation to focus the team, facilitating the major workshop of the meeting, taking down and distributing notes from the meeting, getting the room set up, and clearing the room after the meeting.

Things
That
Take
Effort

COLLABORATIVE TEAMS

"Interdependence *is the paradigm of* we—we *can do it;* we *can cooperate;* we *can combine our talents and abilities and create something greater together.*"
—Covey

Icebreaker Opening Conversation

DESCRIPTION/BACKGROUND

I like to begin a meeting, even if it is only for sixty to ninety minutes, with a short opening conversation. This could be with the entire team as a whole group conversation or by asking each one to turn to the person next to him or her and talk through something briefly. I have used topics related to team concerns, dramatic current events, and general contemporary issues.

Most people walk into a meeting from very hectic, crowded schedules. The icebreaker opening conversation is not so much to break the ice among people who do not know each other as to enable people who do know each other to make the transition to concentrating and attending to what this meeting is going to be about.

In addition, it does provide a moment of personal, one-to-one interaction that can be greatly tension relieving for people who have come from harried responsibilities. The opportunity to spend even a few moments with others sharing some ideas or some experiences can be refreshing for all of us.

I believe that the chance to get connected with the people who are on the team, however briefly, sets the stage for the collaboration and consensus needed as the agenda unfolds.

DID YOU KNOW?

- An icebreaker opening conversation offers the team a bridge to walk over, connecting individual work time to group work time.

- An icebreaker opening conversation can often allow a person just the right chance to release a day's frustration and therefore put more positive energy into the team meeting.

- An icebreaker opening conversation can sometimes raise indirectly the concerns and issues that the team meeting will deal with head-on.

ACTIVITY
#**57**   *Icebreaker Opening*
            Conversation

1. Review for yourself what the particular team task is for this meeting and ask yourself these questions:

   a. Is there a question or topic surrounding this task that comes to mind as an appropriate concern or issue to talk about?

   b. What has the mood of the group been lately? Are there crucial issues or topics that have been weighing it down? What question would allow them a chance to explore their concerns and feelings about that topic?

   c. Is there a current event topic that is taking people's focus and energies?

2. After a one-sentence introduction, pose the question and let people talk in groups of two or three for four or five minutes. Ask for anyone to share a few things talked about. (This allows some of the information to get out but also allows for screening of confidential conversations.)

3. Another option is to pose the question to the whole group and allow a full-group conversation from the start.

4. Within seven to nine minutes, you are ready to move on to the agenda of the meeting with people who have genuinely arrived at the meeting and are now connected to the team.

Hints . . .

✓ **People are not accustomed to this kind of short conversation at the beginning of a task-oriented meeting. Consequently, when you initiate this strategy, be sure to pick safe questions that relate to your agenda.**

✓ **Over time people begin to look forward to these interactions.**

✓ **The success of this strategy depends on the leader's comfort with it and confidence in this strategy's potential for increasing team connection.**

EXAMPLE

The following is a list of different questions I have used with various teams. This activity suggests that you ask just *one* question.

1. What was the best team you have been a part of? What were the qualities that made it so?

2. What is something that has happened recently that made your day?

3. What are some things that concern you about our upcoming major event?

4. When is a time when you had to think quickly "on your feet"?

5. Who do you know who is well organized? What are some of the qualities of a well-organized person? What are some tricks people like that use to be well organized?

6. What have you been learning about our team lately? What are some of our best qualities as a team?

7. How is "_____" (current event) affecting your colleagues? What are some helpful responses one can make?

During a depressing international crisis, I asked this last question of a group, dividing them into pairs to talk about it. When we met back with the whole group, people shared how helpless they had been feeling. When I asked the question— "What are some helpful responses one can make in the midst of such an overwhelming crisis?"— people actually came up with some ways they could respond and at least do something. With that realization the mood shifted and attention could focus on the meeting.

Things
That
Take
Effort
**COLLABORATIVE
TEAMS**

"When people are able to grapple with a difficult and complex problem and come out of it with something far better than could have been had without the joint effort, the emotional reaction is one of deep satisfaction."
—Blake, Mouton, and Allen

Dyad or Triad Brainstorming

DESCRIPTION/BACKGROUND

After a topic or question has been posed and people have had a chance to do some thinking individually, working in groups of two and three to begin talking things through or initial brainstorming together is a critical stage. I have been to meetings where the leader immediately said, "Everyone, this issue has come up. What do you think we should do about it?" Or, "This is my thinking on this issue. What is yours?" The ones who respond are those who have no difficulty speaking up or those who are very quick thinkers. This tends to exclude a lot of us.

By providing time for people to talk things through in smaller groups, you are creating an opportunity for initial team connections and early stages of consensus to happen. This means that the whole burden of creating consensus does not need to fall on the leader's direct interaction with the whole group. Some ideas can be supported or weeded out in this dyad or triad stage.

DID YOU KNOW?

- Some people put more of themselves into a team of two or three than into a larger team.
- Dyads and triads tap the wisdom that often lies untapped in every individual's thinking.
- Some people say things in a group of two or three they do not feel comfortable saying in a larger team.

ACTIVITY

#58

Dyad or Triad Brainstorming

This activity suggests that before you call for discussion from the whole group that you first allow for individual thinking then have discussion in groups of two or three.

1. State the major issue or the question that you want people to think about. You might add a sentence about its significance.

   "Because our company is in a process of restructuring, we need to think through the best way to combine our two divisions and create a model of task realignment. What are the steps you think we need to take in this process?"

2. Share any relevant information.

   "This financial report and market analysis will help you see why this step is important. We are hoping the whole process can be done in under a year."

3. Suggest that people spend three or four minutes thinking individually and writing their own responses.

   "In the next three or four minutes jot down four or five responses from your own thinking about what steps we need to take to combine our two divisions."

4. Have the group divide into mini-teams of two or three to discuss their individual responses.

   "In teams of two or three discuss your responses from your individual thinking. Be ready to share your team's best five or six responses."

5. Then invite the group to share the team's responses either for a brainstormed list on chart paper or on 5 x 8 cards for a full workshop.

Hints . . .

✓ Very often, I just have two or three people who are sitting near each other form the dyad or triad.

✓ If you have been breaking up into these smaller teams many times in one workshop or meeting, then you might have people number off or choose someone from another table to mix up the groups somewhat.

EXAMPLE

One time I worked with a group of four people and gave in to a temptation not to bother with this intermediate step of dyad or triad brainstorming between individual thinking and whole group discussing. The discussion among the four lasted twice as long as any group of thirty or forty would have taken. These days if there are at least four around the table, I make sure we have this mini-team discussion step for it has made the discussion and consensus building part of a meeting go more smoothly and more rapidly.

THINGS
THAT
TAKE
EFFORT

COLLABORATIVE TEAMS

"And unless we value the differences in our perceptions, unless we value each other and give credence to the possibility that we're both right, that life is not always a dichotomous either/ or, that there are almost always third alternatives, we will never be able to transcend the limits of that conditioning."—Covey

Making the Differences Visible

DESCRIPTION/BACKGROUND

In a world of rapid change, teams are discovering that people of many different perspectives, values, and traditions are often thrown together onto a team with the expectation that the members of the team will know how to work in the midst of seemingly irreconcilable perspectives and approaches to handling issues. The most common response to situations like these are denial or overt conflict. Often the denial proceeds until someone or several team members are at an impasse or a breaking point. Then, perhaps without premeditation or warning, a raging conflict ensues.

This activity suggests bringing the differing perspectives to full awareness as a way to start bridging the differences. This activity also assumes that each perspective represented has value and is crucial to the full operation of the team. This activity uses the tool of a graphic organizer, such as a modified Venn diagram, to plot the differences. Following this, appropriate questions can help the group process and reflect on what they have noted.

DID YOU KNOW?

- Denial of differences intensifies their power to be conflicting.
- Becoming aware of differences helps them seem less strange.
- Naming the gifts of these perspectives overtly reminds us of how we need each perspective to make our whole team work.

ACTIVITY

#59 *Making the Differences Visible*

1. If the team has been in conflict, initiate a conversation about what has been going on. Ask: How does conflict usually emerge with us? How do we usually deal with it? What happens to our ability to get the job done when conflict continues?

2. If the team feels that the cause of the conflict lies in the varying views on the team, suggest that they might want to look at these directly.

3. On chart paper, draw three or four large interlocking circles. In the main part of each circle put elements of the perspectives represented on the team. Put the related elements of one perspective within one circle and the elements of a differing perspective in another circle, etc. See the example on the next page. The trick will be to name these elements in objective, nonjudgmental language. When the perspectives are clarified, you might find a way to name the gifts of each perspective.

4. Once the differences have been delineated, push the group to name the ways two perspectives are connected—or what the bridges are between the perspectives.

5. Finally, deal with the intersection of all of the perspectives. What are the points of connections among all of the perspectives represented? What do these suggest are the strengths of our team?

6. At the conclusion of this, step back and ask one or more of the following questions to help the team process what has happened to them:

   a. What observations did you make as we carried out this activity?

   b. What seemed to go smoothly for us? What was difficult for us?

   c. What happened to our team as we went through this activity?

   d. How does this activity enable us to work with our differences?

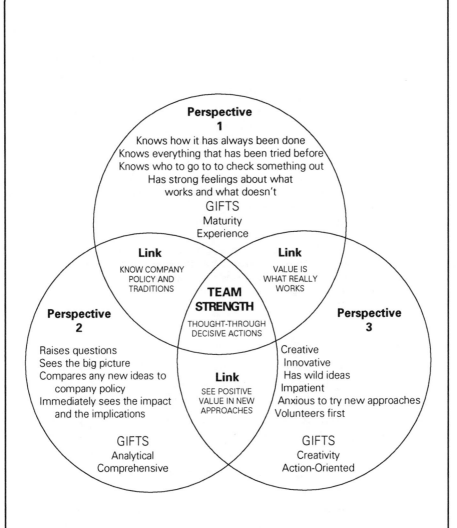

Hints . . .

✓ This is an activity to use either before a conflict has exploded or after a conflict explosion has settled down. This activity will not ease a conflict just after it has exploded.

✓ You might at some time put a humorous name to these perspectives, so that when you run into conflict again in the future you can refer to the conflict in a humorous way and defuse its negative power.

✓ Something like this can be done when dealing with a group representing two or more cultures that are unaccustomed to working together. Gaps seem wider when customs and perspectives are kept hidden. Exposing them to conversation can also expose the values lying underneath these customs. Often these values can be the source of real connection. In other words, look not only at the differing customs but the reasons these customs are used. Some strange customs can make a great deal of sense when the context is understood.

EXAMPLE

One team was having a great deal of difficulty getting along with each other. They hired a consultant to train them in techniques to work through their differences. This consultant suggested the concept of different colored hats. For example, if you are speaking from a visionary, theoretical standpoint, you put on the blue hat while you speak. If you are feeling particularly angry over something, you grab the red hat before you speak. Then, if you are raising some practical, concrete issues or problems, you put on the green hat. Or, if you are clarifying a point, you put on a purple hat, etc. What struck me about this was it very specifically and ingeniously affirmed the gifts of each of those orientations. But more than that, the hats suggested that at different times, we all embody different perspectives.

#60

"Many people have been trained and scripted into defensive and protective communications or into believing that life or other people can't be trusted." —Covey

Team Victory Celebration

DESCRIPTION/BACKGROUND

There are many different ways to hold a team celebration. However it is done, the important thing is to do it. It can be simple or complex. It can be planned or spontaneous. The important thing is to allow celebrations to happen.

There are times when your larger group of twenty or thirty will be celebrating. I also suggest that the smaller team of five to ten can celebrate from time to time in some appropriate way. At this level, elaborateness is not necessary. Simplicity and the fact that celebrations happen are important.

Celebrations send a message to team members that they are worthwhile and effective. By breaking the routine, celebrations sustain motivation for the long haul.

DID YOU KNOW?

- Even little celebrations feed the spirit of the team.
- Celebrations connect people in different ways than discussions and team-work.
- Variety in celebrations adds zest and excitement to the life of the team.

ACTIVITY

#60   *Team Victory Celebration*

When I hold a celebration these are the critical elements I try to include. The setting can be a regular team meeting or part of a celebrative meal.

1. A time for the teams to list their victories and accomplishments.

2. Some place for the teams to list for everybody or show everyone all of their accomplishments.

3. A chance for each team to read their list of accomplishments.

4. An opportunity for anyone else to add to the list for each particular team area.

5. A chance to step back and reflect on the impact of this information on victories and accomplishments. Some of these questions might be helpful:

   a. What victories surprised you?

   b. Which ones had you forgotten?

   c. Which ones particularly pleased you?

   d. Which ones were easy to accomplish? Harder to accomplish?

   e. What is the new position we are now in because of these accomplishments?

   f. What does this say our next steps need to be?

Hints . . .

✓ The day-to-day operation of teams makes it quite difficult to keep your attention on things that might be going well.

✓ A celebration could be a regular occurrence at the end of a specific time period such as a quarter or half-year. A celebration could be a spontaneous occurrence at the end of a particularly long project, or it could be at the announcement that a proposal has been accepted, or a team has just received an award.

✓ Celebrations are something different than the usual day-to-day routine.

EXAMPLE

Some celebrations I have seen are:

One group celebrated the end of the first three months of its plan with a potluck lunch.

One team celebrated the end of a project by going to a movie together.

A school celebrated getting off the state at-risk list by inviting the governor to come and speak.

Some companies celebrate a team's victory with the manager or chief executive officer taking them to lunch.

Some companies send winning teams on a paid vacation!

Another team celebrated by witnessing a new technological advance that could streamline its work.

COLLABORATIVE TEAMS

ENHANCING GROUP REFLECTION

INTRODUCTION TO REFLECTION

Reflection is the opportunity to step back and think about what you have been doing, how you have been doing it, and what has been going on with the people you have been doing it with. Many people today are calling it the "processing" part of a meeting or an event.

Reflection is a time of connecting. This allows people an opportunity to connect what has been happening with other ideas or other experiences they have had at other times of their lives. It gives people a chance to connect with each other through thoughts and feelings heretofore unexpressed. It also provides an opportunity to articulate areas in which they have been struggling.

When this happens, you increase exponentially the potential for deep consensus within a group. People who feel this connected can see places and possibilities for agreement that normally would go unnoticed or unimagined. Consequently, enhancing group reflection has a very deep and profound impact on the ability of a group to create and expand authentic consensus.

"When you communicate synergistically, you are simply opening your mind and heart and expressions to new possibilities, new alternatives, new options." —Covey

Content Processing

DESCRIPTION/BACKGROUND

When a presentation has been made, it can be quite helpful to step back a moment and see what people remember and have absorbed through a content-processing conversation. Perhaps a video has just been shown, the group has just heard a speaker, or you asked everyone to read an article before coming to the meeting. Holding this conversation can tell you as the facilitator what aspects need to be rehearsed again and which aspect of the material has already been well absorbed. This is the opportunity for people to make the material their own by connecting it to their own thoughts and experiences.

This is also an opportunity for individuals to expand their initial comprehension of the material with the insights and connections other people have made with the information.

DID YOU KNOW?

- Content processing helps people make the information presented their very own information.
- Content processing helps people translate the information presented into the situations of their own daily lives.
- Content processing reveals to everyone the different ways other people in the group are making sense of the information presented.

ACTIVITY

#**61**   *Content Processing*

This activity highlights a way to hold a guided discussion on a data presentation that has just been made.

1. Before hearing the talk or seeing the video, you might say a word to the group underlining the significance of the topic and alerting them to note things of interest to share afterward in a guided discussion.

2. Choose several of these questions listed below, keeping this basic flow.

    a. What words or phrases do you recall from the presentation? (If it is a video presentation, what objects or scenes do you remember?)

    b. What were some of the key ideas or main points in the presentation?

    c. Where did you get interested or intrigued? Where were you surprised?

    d. What points seemed difficult to grasp? With which ideas did you struggle?

    e. What aspects of the material made sense to you out of your own experience?

    f. Looking at this presentation as a whole, what are some of the most important messages communicated?

    g. What are some questions this has sparked in your mind?

    h. Who else needs to hear or see this presentation?

    i. What are some of the implications for us?

3. Allow several responses to each question before moving to the next.

4. After about fifteen minutes move to the next item on the meeting agenda.

Hints . . .

✓ Note the way that the progression of questions enhances participation.

✓ Perhaps you might be tempted to skip questions a, b, and c because they appear simple and elementary. Beginning with these questions helps to make sure that everyone is starting from the same objective information.

✓ You might remember conversations you have had which began with question e, f, or g. Some groups may have difficulty jumping into a conversation at that depth or may even jump in with perspectives that have ignored some of the basic information reviewed in earlier questions. Then your conversation ends up pulling people apart rather than bringing them together.

✓ As with other conversations suggested in this book, it is not necessary to have a comprehensive screen of answers before you move on to the next question. The flow of the questions has set up a reflective process whether people respond out loud or not.

EXAMPLE

Before leading a planning session for a major corporation on improving their strategies for customer service, the meeting planners showed a video made by their competitor about how they carried out customer service. Showing the expert ways their competitor cared for the customer certainly got the attention of everyone. But spending twenty minutes in content processing allowed people to make direct application both to customer service practices they thought were satisfactory as well as to those they were clear needed improvement.

"Getting the maximum benefits from commitment, involvement, strong initiative, good inquiry, open advocacy, effective conflict resolution, solid decision making, and extensive use of critique is what spectacular teamwork is all about." —Blake, Mouton, and Allen

Meeting Processing

DESCRIPTION/BACKGROUND

No matter how much time is left, stepping back and processing the meeting is absolutely critical in helping the group to see the full importance of the meeting. Meeting processing can enable the participants to connect with the larger significance of the meeting and its accomplishments or decisions. Furthermore, it provides an opportunity for the meeting to end and the transition to next activities or tasks to occur.

If you have had a one-hour meeting, ideally you could spend three or four minutes processing the meeting. However, even if you have only thirty seconds you can pose a question and get three or four responses.

DID YOU KNOW?

- Meeting processing helps people make sense of the details of a meeting.
- Meeting processing allows people to see the value of the time they have just spent together.
- People's whole impressions of a meeting can be changed positively when they hear other people's ideas about what has just happened.

ACTIVITY

#**62**   *Meeting Processing*

This activity illustrates one way to lead a short directed conversation immediately following a team meeting.

1. Complete all initial announcements and settle the next meeting time.

2. Then suggest to the group that all of you spend two or three minutes stepping back from the meeting and "debriefing."

3. Choose two or three of these questions and allow a few answers to each before moving to the next.

   a. What have we accomplished during our meeting today?

   b. What was helpful for you personally today?

   c. Where did you, or where did we, struggle in this meeting?

   d. What were things that we did that helped us reach these accomplishments?

   e. How would you improve the way we hold a meeting?

   f. How would you tell someone else what really happened in this meeting today?

4. Close the meeting appropriately—e.g., by thanking everyone for their participation.

Hints . . .

✓ There are many ways of stepping back and processing. The trick is creating the variety so that people do not tire of this step.

✓ The length of time spent on processing is not as crucial as the honoring of this dynamic.

✓ In time, you might be able to get your group to reflect on the importance of these very processing questions.

EXAMPLE

I worked with a teacher who had created a list of twenty-five possible processing questions. When it came time to process the session just completed, she had a wealth of questions at her fingertips. I have modified her questions slightly. They include:

How easy or difficult was it for us to get started? Why?
How much of our meeting was on track? Off track? What does that tell us?
What has this meeting reminded you of?
Describe the mental and physical activities that took place during our meeting. At what moments did you feel most anxious or stressed?
What factors seem to affect the quality of our meeting?
What is the next stage in the development of meetings that work?

In a lighter vein, I have asked, "If we were to set this meeting to music, what kind of music might that be?" Some responses have been:

"I'd set it to jazz because some of the parts were confusing and then it came together."

"I'd set it to symphony music because everything was harmonious."

"I'd set it to rock and roll because it was lively and fun."

FOR
THE
COMMITTED

COLLABORATIVE
TEAMS

"You begin with the belief that parties involved will gain more insight, and that the excitement of that mutual learning and insight will create a momentum toward more and more insights, learnings, and growth."—Covey

Teamwork Processing

DESCRIPTION/BACKGROUND

When people are first learning to work together in a team, it may be useful from time to time to reflect on how well the teams are operating. This can give teams clues as to how to improve their work together. With the heavy emphasis our culture has given to individualism, it is important to find ways to smooth out and encourage the team formation process.

Another time this conversation might be useful is when a team or teams seem to be having problems working together. This could provide an opportunity for the team to diagnose some of its issues or problems, thereby giving it a chance to create its own solutions.

DID YOU KNOW?

- A well-functioning team does not just happen—it takes hard work to perfect.
- Teamwork processing can help a team make its own adjustments in order to perform more effectively.
- The more teamwork processing happens, the more skill and sophistication a team can develop to process its current situation, as well as its next phases of growth.

MORE THAN 50 WAYS

ACTIVITY
#63 *Teamwork Processing*

This activity suggests that every few meetings the team leader find some appropriate ways to process how the dynamics of the teamwork are going. Therefore the focus of the questions is on the team itself.

1. Get all extraneous announcements completed as well as mention the date and time of the next meeting.

2. Then suggest that the group spend four or five minutes checking in to see how its teamwork is progressing.

3. Choosing several of the following questions, lead a directed conversation.

   a. What were some of our team's accomplishments today?

   b. What are some things our team did today that displayed helpful teamwork?

   c. What are some things our team did that enabled the task to get done today?

   d. What did you appreciate about the work of our team today?

   e. How did our team work through things that first appeared as blocks to its teamwork?

   f. What are some things our team could do differently in its approach to a task or that would improve its work as a team?

   g. What has our team taught you about what genuine teamwork is all about?

4. If the team wants to spend time on a concern or issue, follow the team's lead. Try to guide the team to a resolution or concrete decision if that seems possible in the short time you have. Otherwise suggest spending more time on this at a succeeding team meeting.

5. Close the conversation and the meeting appropriately.

Hints . . .

✓ Obviously, this is not a conversation you hold every time a team meets. After the group has met a few times, it might be helpful. It might also be helpful at the end of a time period, such as a quarter or semester. The key is using methods that help the team to figure out on its own how to improve its workings and how to appreciate what it is doing well. It is helpful to hold this kind of conversation long before an explosive blow-up. This conversation is a better preventive strategy than a reparative strategy.

✓ For your regular meetings, a one-question processing is all you might have time for.

✓ In addition to opportunities for processing and reflection, some teams may need some concrete suggestions to help them build skills in conflict resolution, attentive listening, and so on.

EXAMPLE

When I was responsible for a team engaged in a highly complex project with which few had any previous experience, I found it necessary to hold these conversations frequently. These conversations taught me several things. First, I got clues about how confident the team members were feeling about the team's ability to get the job done. Second, I was able to discern who was working well with whom or who was not working well with whom. Third, I could tell what tasks needed to be altered or whose assignments needed to be shifted to enable the work to get done. By the end of the project the team was operating as a cohesive and confident unit.

"Most of the self-improvement material puts independence on a pedestal, as though communication, teamwork, and cooperation were lesser values." —Covey

Logs or Journals

DESCRIPTION/BACKGROUND

Another way to occasion the processing dynamic is through logs or journals. In other words, you could decide to conclude some team meetings with three or four minutes of writing in a log or a journal instead of holding a processing conversation out loud. You could provide the journals or sheets for people to put into their journals later. The key to this is what works for your group. You are suggesting indirectly, by the way, that a log or a journal is helpful on an individual basis as a way to step back and reflect on personal life issues, too.

DID YOU KNOW?

- An opportunity to write allows some people to organize their thoughts in a way that conversations do not.
- Writing encourages people to express thoughts and feelings they might never say out loud.
- Logs and journals can be a tool for mental refreshment.

ACTIVITY

#64 *Logs or Journals*

This activity sets aside a few minutes for people to write about things they are learning or experiencing in the work of the team.

1. Say a few words about the importance of writing and stepping back to look at what you are experiencing.

2. Provide team members with blank paper or a form with some questions to guide their thinking.

3. Suggest team members spend four or five minutes writing.

4. Before closing, ask if one or two people might read one or two of the sentences they have written.

5. Thank everyone and close the meeting.

Hints . . .

✓ Some people begin a log or journal and adhere to it quite regularly. Others begin it for a while, break off, and begin again. It is crucial to avoid making this into a rule or a law. Logs and journals can be helpful activities. They are not meant to be kept just for their own sake.

✓ Some people may find it helpful to put only pictures or images in their journals.

✓ After people have written in their journals, I have often asked if two or three people would share a sentence or two they have written. In addition to the individual impact this activity has, some extremely powerful reflections have been occasioned and shared through this tool.

EXAMPLE

Some people who organized a conference for school principals decided that this kind of reflective activity was so important that they bought each principal participant a small blank book to be used as a log or journal. Then once or twice each day of the conference they provided time for the principals to write in them.

You may also want to provide a way to return a few days later to something members have written and see what other ideas, insights, or reflections occur after several days have passed.

65

"Interdependence is a choice only independent people can make. Dependent people cannot choose to become interdependent. They don't have the character to do it; they don't own enough of themselves." —Covey

Career Motivation Conversation

DESCRIPTION/BACKGROUND

This conversation is to help group members talk together about their deep and profound motivations for doing what they are doing. In the rush of daily tasks, these reminders are hard to talk about and at times, especially in the midst of crises, difficult to remember. A conversation that can help people articulate the motivations behind their career decisions feeds the spirits of everyone present.

Although this conversation is not an antidote to total group cynicism, it can be a booster in the midst of temporary group discouragement.

DID YOU KNOW?

- Human beings need constant reminders as to the deeper reasons why they have chosen their careers.
- The day-to-day grind quickly focuses people away from the deeper significance of their careers.
- Career motivating conversations can feed the human spirit.

ACTIVITY

#65   *Career Motivation Conversation*

This guided discussion will take about fifteen or twenty minutes and provides people an opportunity to talk about some of their deeper career motivations. Use this with a team that has been meeting a while. You might introduce a full planning session with this conversation.

1. Begin with some easy questions.

    a. How long have all of you been at this work? Let's go around the room and hear the number of years from each person.

    b. Who has been doing this the longest? The shortest?

    c. What roles or assignments have you enjoyed the most? Why?

    d. What roles or assignments have you enjoyed the least? Why?

2. Then shift to some more serious questions.

    a. In what moments or occasions have you been tempted to throw in the towel and do something else?

    b. In those times, what have you told yourself or what reminders have you given yourself that have kept you returning to this work?

    c. What word of advice would you like to pass on to those who are just beginning this kind of career?

3. Two or three profound answers to either 2b or 2c would be great. Once that has happened find a way to close smoothly, thanking people for sharing their thoughts.

Hints . . .

✓ While each person is mentioning the number of years he or she has been doing this work, you might assign someone to write down these numbers and add them up. It is impressive to hear the total number of years a group has spent engaged in its careers.

✓ Although this is a very serious conversation, there can be moments of laughter to help people deal with the intensity of the responses.

✓ People are interested in hearing about times when their colleagues wanted to quit and give up. They become open and ready to hear what has kept people returning to their jobs.

✓ Deciding the right moment for a group to experience this conversation is one of the most difficult aspects about this activity.

EXAMPLE

Recently I met with a team that had been meeting a lot of opposition to their work. They had met frequently, created lots of plans, had actually had several successes, but were not experiencing a lot of external support.

Out of the blue one of the team members asked, "Why do you suppose we keep doing this?" I had not planned this activity for this group at this particular moment, but here it was happening. I stopped my leading of the meeting and listened to the comments unfold.

"I do this because I enjoy planning new things."

"I do this because I appreciate working with other people."

"I do this because I want to make a difference."

"I do this because I believe our community needs it."

"I do this because the future is depending on efforts like mine."

In a few moments people became aware of the big picture once again. It was as if they had been refreshed and were ready to work.

CONCLUSION

B y now, the truth is out. Consensus is a long, careful process. There are some things you can do right now to move your group toward consensus. However, your skill as a leader is called on to decide what this group can come to a consensus on. There are some things you can ask someone to do the first day on the job. There are other things you do not ask them to do until they have been on the job for a year. Some victories can happen right away, and they should be celebrated. With patience, deeper and more complicated points of consensus can be reached.

It may also be clearer that on the road to consensus conflicts are inevitable. Even with the most skilled facilitation and the most careful of processes, conflicts will emerge. Though at the time it is hard to have confidence in this, a conflict can be an opportunity. A conflict may be a sign that your team is deepening or expanding its vision. In this way, conflicts can point the way to a larger, more comprehensive vision.

I have just two messages in closing. In the midst of the journey to consensus, one of your jobs as leader is to continue helping to make the thinking of the group visible. Groups often get derailed when they forget or ignore the thinking they have done so far and the thinking they are doing right at the moment. That is why writing things on chart paper or cards has been emphasized in this book. It is also why I suggest that as a leader you do your own writing of how things are going, continually reflecting on how things can be improved, and how doing something a little differently might help your group have a breakthrough. Your own log and record of your group's victories and turning points can remind you of how far it has come.

The second message is a reminder of the crucial role of your teams. The more you encourage the teams, and the more you offer them responsibility and trust, the more opportunities they will have to show their strength and creativity. This then allows you as leader to be more of a coach and facilitator rather than the manager.

I welcome hearing from you about what is working, what is not working, how you have improved on some of the suggestions in this book, and finally, how you have created something entirely new, perhaps sparked by some of the material here.

BIBLIOGRAPHY

Adams, J. D. (Ed.). (1986). *Transforming leadership: From vision to results.* Alexandria, VA: Miles River Press.

Adams, J. D. (Ed.). (1984). *Transforming work: A collection of organizational transformation readings.* Alexandria, VA: Miles River Press.

Axelrod, R. (1984). *The evolution of cooperation.* New York: Basic Books, Inc., Publishers.

Baker, P. J., Curtis, D., & Beneson, W. (1991). *Collaborative opportunities to build better schools.* Normal, IL: Illinois Association for Supervision and Curriculum Development.

Baldwin, B. A. (1993, January). The morale fiber. *USAir Magazine*, p. 16-20.

Blake, R. R., Mouton, J. S., & Allen, R. L. (1987). *Spectacular teamwork: How to develop the leadership skills for team success.* New York: John Wiley & Sons.

Bolton, R. (1979). *People skills: How to assert yourself, listen to others, and resolve conflicts.* Englewood Cliffs, NJ: Prentice-Hall, Inc.

Boulding, K. E. (1966). *The image.* Ann Arbor, MI: University of Michigan Press.

Costa, A.L. (1991). *The school as a home for the mind.* Palatine, IL: IRI/Skylight Publishing, Inc.

Covey, S. R. (1990). *The 7 habits of highly effective people: Powerful lessons in personal change.* New York: Simon & Schuster Inc.

Fogarty, R., & Bellanca, J. (1989). *Patterns for thinking: Patterns for transfer.* Palatine, IL: IRI/Skylight Publishing, Inc.

Gardner, H. (1983). *Frames of mind: The theory of multiple intelligences.* New York: HarperCollins Publishers.

Gerstein, A., & Reagan, J. (1986). *Win-win: Approaches to conflict resolution.* Salt Lake City: Gibbs M. Smith, Inc.

Institute of Cultural Affairs. (1981). Imaginal training methods. *Image: A Journal on the Human Factor.* Chicago: Author.

Institute of Cultural Affairs. (1973). *5th city preschooling institute: An experiment in early education.* Chicago: Author.

237

Johnson, D. W., & Johnson, R. T. (1988, May). Critical thinking through structured controversy. *Educational Leadership*, p. 58-64.

Lazear, D. (1991a). *Seven ways of knowing: Teaching for multiple intelligences.* Palatine, IL: IRI/Skylight Publishing, Inc.

Lazear, D. (1991b). *Seven ways of teaching: The artistry of teaching with multiple intelligences.* Palatine, IL: IRI/Skylight Publishing, Inc.

Lindsay, W. M., Curtis, R. K., & Manning, G. E. (1989, June). A participative management primer. *Journal for Quality and Participation*, p. 78-84.

Lipset, S. M. (1985). *Consensus and conflict: Essays in political sociology.* New Brunswick, NJ: Transaction Books.

Mansbridge, J. J. (Ed.). (1990). *Beyond self-interest.* Chicago: The University of Chicago Press.

Naisbitt, J. (1982). *Megatrends.* New York: Warner Books.

Owen, H. (1987). *Spirit: Transformation and development in organizations.* Potomac, MD: Abbott Publishing.

Partridge, P. H. (1971). *Consent & consensus.* New York: Praeger Publishers.

Peters, T. (1987). *Thriving on chaos: Handbook for a management revolution.* New York: Alfred A. Knopf.

Russell, P. (1983). *The global brain.* Los Angeles: J. P. Tarcher.

Scearce, C. (1992). *100 ways to build teams.* Palatine, IL: IRI/Skylight Publishing, Inc.

Seldman, M. (1986). *Self-talk: The winning edge in selling.* Granville, OH: Performance Systems Press.

Senge, P. M. (1990). *The fifth discipline: The art and practice of the learning organization.* New York: Doubleday Currency.

Sher, B., & Gottlieb, A. (1989). *Teamworks!: Building support groups that guarantee success.* New York: Warner Books.

Sizer, T. R. (1991, May). No pain, no gain. *Educational Leadership*, p. 32-34.

Spencer, L. J. (1989). *Winning through participation.* Dubuque, IA: Kendall/Hunt Publishing Company.

Thompson, B. L. (1991, June). Negotiation training: Win-win or what? *Training*, p. 31-35.

Townsend, P. L., & Gebhardt, J. E. (1989, June). Try continuous involvement improvement. *Journal for Quality and Participation*, p. 18-21.

Umpleby, S. A. (1991). Methods for making social organizations adaptive. In De Zeeuw, G. & Glanville, R. (Eds.). *Collective support systems and their users* (p. 155-162). Amsterdam, The Netherlands: Thesis Publishers.

Umpleby, S. A. (1983). A group process approach to organizational change. In Wedde, H. (Ed.) *Adequate modeling of systems* (p. 116- 125). New York: Springer-Verlag.

Wynn, R., & Guditus, C. W. (1984). *Team management: Leadership by consensus.* Columbus, OH: Charles E. Merrill Publishing Company.

Zenger, J. H. (1985, December). Leadership: Management's better half. *Training*, p. 44-53.

INDEX

Connection
  increasing supportive, 195
  dyad or triad brainstorming in, 208–10
  icebreaker opening conversation in,
    204–7
  leadership rotation in, 200–3
  making differences visible in, 211–14
  team victory celebration in, 215–17
  winning team story in, 196–99
Consensus, 1
  building, viii, 175
  definition of, ix
  need for tools, viii
  setting and logistics for team, ix–x
  team approach to, viii–ix
Content processing, 219–21
Conversations. See also Communication
  career motivation, 231–33
  common direction written summary in,
    18–20
  content processing, 219–21
  global events, 47–50
  hopes and desires, 5–8
  icebreaker opening, 204–7
  implementation learning, 161–63
  language in, 75–77
  nervousness about, 158–60
  specific praise in, 138–40
  TV personality in three years in, 15–17
Cooperative writing workshop, 109–11
Covey, S. R., 5, 28, 125, 155, 172, 173, 179,
    192, 204, 211, 215, 219, 225,
    228, 231
Creativity
  spontaneous, 78

Direction, 4. See also Common direction
    visualization
Documentation, visible, 24
  articles in, 40–42
  artifacts in, 31–33
  cardstorming in, 25–27
  meeting products documentation in,
    28–30
  reports in, 34–36
  wall decor of meeting products in, 37–39
Dyad brainstorming, 208–10

Eventful happenings, 69–71

Feedback, project, 144–46
Framework. See Total framework illumina-
    tion
Future, focus on, in hopes and desires
    conversation, 6–8

Gardner, Howard, 25
Global events conversation, 47–50

Group agreements, 101–2
  cooperative writing workshop in,
    109–11
  mapping road to, 112–14
  organization principles workshop in,
    54–56
  stating and restating, 115–17
  three-to-one scenarios in, 106–8
  workshop flow in, 103–5
Group mind, 173
Group think, 173
Guided conversation. See Conversations

Hopes and desires conversation, 5–8

Icebreaker opening conversation, 204–7
Imaging. See also Brainstorming
  journey wall in, 44–46
  past, present, and future in, 21–23
  snapshots in, 9–11
  TV personality in three years in, 15–17
Implementation learning conversation,
    161–63
Individual celebrations, 141–43
Individual commitment, x, 119–20
  eliciting detailed assignments, 121–36
    assignment chart, 134–36
    attendance, 131–33
    task volunteers, 122–24
    timelines, 128–30
    what/who/when cards, 125–27
  expanding personal recognition, 137–52
    individual celebrations in, 141–43
    personalized job tools in, 150–52
    specific praise in, 138–40
    training, coaching, or project
      feedback in, 144–46
    usage of people's names in, 147–49
  occasioning individual accountability/
      absolution, 153–69
    implementation learning conversation
      in, 161–63
    meeting length in, 155–57
    nervousness about conversations in,
      158–60
    as symbol of commitment in, 167–69
    victory party in, 164–66

Job tools, personalized, 150–52
Journals, writing in, 228–30
Journey wall, 44–46

Language, 75–77. See also Communication;
    Conversations; Questions; Writing
Leadership rotation, 200–3
Left brain, 78
List of team members, 176–78
Logs, writing in, 228–30

240

242

There are
one-story intellects,
two-story intellects, and three-story
intellects with skylights. All fact collectors who have
no aim beyond their facts are one-story men. Two-story men
compare, reason, generalize, using the labors of the fact collectors as
well as their own. Three-story men idealize, imagine,
predict—their best illumination comes
from above, through the skylight.
—*Oliver Wendell*
Holmes